LEGENDARY LIGHTHOUSES

LEGENDARY LIGHTHOUSES

THE COMPANION TO THE
PBS TELEVISION SERIES

John Grant and Ray Jones

The
Globe
Pequot
Press

Old Saybrook, Connecticut

Other Lighthouse Books Published by
THE GLOBE PEQUOT PRESS

American Lighthouses

California Lighthouses: Point St. George to the Gulf of Santa Catalina

Eastern Great Lakes Lighthouses: Ontario, Erie, and Huron

Gulf Coast Lighthouses: Florida Keys to the Rio Grande

Mid-Atlantic Lighthouses: Hudson River to Chesapeake Bay

New England Lighthouses: Bay of Fundy to Long Island Sound

Pacific Northwest Lighthouses: Oregon, Washington, Alaska, and British Columbia

Southeastern Lighthouses: Outer Banks to Cape Florida

Western Great Lakes Lighthouses: Michigan and Superior

Cover design by Bill Brown
Cover photo by Bruce Roberts
Text design by Laura Augustine
All photos are by Bruce Roberts unless otherwise credited.

Library of Congress Cataloging-in-Publication Data
Grant, John, 1948-
    Legendary lighthouses : the companion to the PBS television series / John Grant and
      Ray Jones. —1st ed.
             p.   cm.
    Includes index.
    ISBN 0-7627-0325-3
    1. Lighthouses—United States.   2. Lighthouse Keepers—United States.   I. Jones,
    Ray, 1948- . II. Legendary lighthouses (Television program)   III. Title.
VK1023.G73   1998
387.1'55'0973—dc21

                                                       98-34417
                                                         CIP

Printed in Canada
First Edition / Third Printing

For Joan and Andy
    —*John Grant*

For my dear friends Bruce Roberts and Cheryl Shelton-Roberts
    —*Ray Jones*

Acknowledgments

The *Legendary Lighthouses* book and television series could not have been created without the help of the hundreds of individuals who are actively involved in the care and preservation of lighthouses across the United States. These individuals, many of whom make it into the pages of this book, are part of an amazing grassroots effort to save America's lighthouses. They provided incredible logistical help, getting us to locations by plane and boat that we would otherwise not have been able to reach. We rarely made a request that wasn't met with a smile and a suggestion of how to get it done.

We want to thank the U.S. Coast Guard for their logistical and transportation support. There was always a coastguardsman waiting with a key, even at the remotest lighthouse tower.

Since this book started as a television series, we must acknowledge the contributions of the people who produced the television programs. The work done by producers David Oyster, Jeff Streich, and Jack McDonald provided invaluable insights and creativity for the book.

The photographs in the book that are taken from the actual television programs provide only a small hint of the quality of the work done by the videographers for the television series. They are Peter Nelson, Don Hampton, Ken Allison and Jeff Streich. We are also grateful for the excellent work done by Judson P. Mantz in selecting and transferring the video shots for use in the book.

We are thankful to be able to include in the book the majestic lighthouse photos of Bruce Roberts. Bruce and his wife, Cheryl, are great friends of lighthouses, and we are thankful to them for their willingness to help with this book.

Funding provided by PBS helped to make this entire project possible. We are grateful for the support and confidence of PBS programming executives Kathy Quattrone and John Wilson and for the feedback and support provided by PBS staffers Mary Jane McKinven and Steven Gray.

We owe a debt of gratitude to our coproduction colleagues at WPSX-TV, Penn State. General manager Mark Erstling saw the potential of the project and made it happen. WPSX staffers Mark Smukler and Tracy Vosburgh Frieden put tremendous amounts of time and energy into making the television series and the book realities.

As a first time author, I am very thankful to have landed in the comforting and capable hands of two publishing veterans. Ray Jones has written some of America's most popular lighthouse books. He was a joy to work with in writing this book.

Laura Strom, the executive editor at Globe Pequot, was an early advocate of the book. She worked tirelessly to make the book better. She also served as a wonderful guide through the world of book publishing, always willing to answer or explain even the most basic aspects of publishing to a novice author.

I have always wanted to write a book to be able to acknowledge the two people without whom none of this would be worth doing—my wife, Joan, and son, Andy.

John Grant
Driftwood Productions

Contents

What Is It About Lighthouses?

Every purposeful journey must be guided by a beacon, however faint. When we began work on the *Legendary Lighthouses* PBS television series some years ago, it was apparent that we were setting out on a quest of sorts. Our intent was to celebrate lighthouses as travel destinations, active aids to navigation, and historic monuments. But we knew we would be probing some deeper meanings as well, for lighthouses are no ordinary structures. They speak to people on many levels. They evoke powerful emotional responses, even in those who live hundreds of miles from the sea and have never had to rely on them for help in reaching a safe harbor. To find out why this is so, we traveled the U.S. coasts from Downeast Maine to Key West, Florida; from San Diego to Seattle; from Chicago to Duluth, Minnesota. We trekked thousands of miles by land, water, and air and visited scores of lighthouses, some of them so remote that they could be reached only by helicopter.

Legendary Lighthouses film crew in the Pacific Northwest

What is it about lighthouses? Neither the television series nor this book attempts to answer that question directly. Perhaps you can answer it for yourself once you've experienced *Legendary Lighthouses*.

Both the series and the book take a people-oriented, storytelling approach to their subject. They are not meant to serve as encyclopedias of technical or historical data on particular lighthouses. Although you'll get plenty of information on the basics of present-day and historic lighthouse technology, you won't always be told the height of a tower or how many individual steps are in the spiral staircase leading to its lantern room.

On the other hand, you *will* find out what maritime museum director John Olguin said when he learned of the plan to bulldoze California's Point Fermin Lighthouse (page 134) and how teenager Abbie Burgess and her family survived the tidal wave that swept over their island light station off the coast of Maine in 1856 (page 58). You will learn how a three-ton glass lens is being reassembled piece by piece at the Navesink Lighthouse in New Jersey (page 34) and how a Coast Guard Aids to Navigation team in Washington State has made the Cape Flattery Lighthouse more effective by painting its windows black (page 150). And you'll dis-

Sunrise at **Cape Hatteras**

Photo by Jeff Streich

The **Cape Flattery Light** warns tankers away from Washington's rugged and environmentally sensitive Olympic Peninsula.

cover how a nineteenth-century Cape Florida keeper got down from the top of his light tower after a Seminole war party burned the wooden steps out from under him (page 101) and how Boy Scouts are rolling up their sleeves to save decaying lighthouses in the Western Great Lakes (page 192).

To get to the heart of these stories, we rely on local storytellers with close links to navigational lights and the sea. We speak to ordinary people who have some extraordinary things to say about lighthouses. You'll hear from them in the following pages. You'll also see them, because we've included many stills of live shots from the television production. Keep in mind that action shots pulled from television footage won't look quite the same as the bright, colorful photographs we've used to illustrate some of the lighthouses.

Nearly every person we met and interviewed on camera was asked the question: What is it about lighthouses? Astoundingly, the answers we got were like fingerprints. No two were the same. In the end, we found that the answers—like people's relationships with the lighthouses themselves—were always personal.

One of our favorite responses comes from Peter Ralston of Maine, who helps us grasp the larger meaning lighthouses have even for people who have never seen or made use of one. "People get what lighthouses are about," he says. "Lighthouses speak to vigilance. They speak to caring. They speak to being there. They speak to helping other human beings."

Inevitably, our search carried us to people who actually lived in lighthouses and to some who still do. In large part, the lighthouse saga is a family story. At most U.S. light stations before automation, the wives and children of the keepers lived at the lighthouses and shared much of the workload. In fact, the U.S. Lighthouse Service preferred hiring

Peter Ralston

2

Cameraman on the Mackinac Bridge

married keepers, knowing full well that family members would be valuable—usually unpaid—assets in maintaining these essential aids to navigation.

Cheryl Roberts, who coauthored the book *Lighthouse Families*, was a fountain of information about the families who called lighthouses their home. Incidentally, Cheryl's coauthor and husband, Bruce, is the source of many of the lighthouse photographs in this book. Cheryl pointed us to the children of dozens of old-time keepers.

Despite the hardships of life at remote light stations, these children have amazingly fond memories of growing up in lighthouses.

The six daughters of keeper William Owens grew up during the late 1930s and 1940s at California's Point Arena Lighthouse, which sits on a lonely cliff overlooking the Pacific. Three of the sisters returned to Point Arena with us to be interviewed for the television series.

"My dad taught us to turn the light on," remembers Sarah Owens Schwartz. "We all had to do that. But it was just a job to us and a home. I never thought about what it was doing for the ships. It was just our life."

"You don't realize the importance of it or the beauty of it until you get older and move away from it," recalls Diana Owens Brown, the youngest of the six sisters.

Adds Shirlee Owens Storms, "When I look back on it, I'd say we had a very good life. I wish we could get back to it."

Getting back to it is what a lot of us are doing these days. People are visiting lighthouses in record numbers. This is true partly because the old towers and dwellings remind us of a bygone era when life was quieter and simpler—or so we like to believe. But it is true also because, located in lovely, oceanside settings, lighthouses make fabulous travel destinations.

Our lighthouse travels took us to such spectacularly beautiful and popular areas as

The **Outer Island Light** station in Wisconsin's Apostle Islands.

LEGENDARY LIGHTHOUSES

Cape Cod, the Chesapeake Bay, the North Carolina Outer Banks, New York's famed Fire Island, the pristine Apostle Islands of Lake Superior, Washington's San Juan Islands, California's Big Sur, and the Florida Keys. In the chapters that follow, you'll go with us to these and many other wondrous locales.

What sets these destinations apart from many others is a strong sense of place. Cape Cod's Greg O'Brien understands this. "It's bigger than all of us," he says. "It's spectacular. It's beautiful, and we're all attracted to it."

Highly suggestive of that sense of wonderment are the Cape's several working lighthouses. While people flock to Cape Cod to enjoy its beaches and natural beauty, they also go there to see its historic light towers. In fact, lighthouses have become an emblem of the Cape just as they have for many other coastal destinations.

Lighthouses are now prime tourist attractions. They house maritime museums as well as beachside shops, galleries, and bookstores. A few serve as charming bed and breakfast inns, where people can have the ultimate lighthouse experience by actually staying in an old keeper's residence.

But lighthouses are more than mere symbols, more than just antique buildings of interest to curious tourists. They still have an active role to play in the commercial and maritime life of the nation. Although no longer as critical to navigation as they once were, they still serve the needs of mariners, especially local fishermen and recreational boaters. And they are available to guide larger vessels when satellite location-finding equipment and other modern electronic gadgets go on the blink.

It was the practical usefulness of lighthouses that caused them to be built in the first place. In addition to saving lives and property, lighthouses stimulated trade. Port cities that built early lighthouses, such as Boston (1716) and New York (1769), got a head start on other coastal communities in commercial development. So throughout much of our nation's history, lighthouses were thought of as tools of commerce and industry.

Brant Point, Nantucket

For these and other reasons, our current romantic notions about lighthouses should be balanced against some harder-edged historical and social realities. Lighthouses were built and maintained at considerable human and financial cost. A keeper's job was hard, and it could be dangerous. The lives of keepers were much more like those of industrial workers than of poets.

To bring these realities into focus, we'll introduce you to some true-to-life

John Tregembo at Rock of Ages

The **Bodie Island Lighthouse** stands amid this
otherwordly Outer Banks sunset. Rising 166 feet
above sea level, the tower holds a giant first-order
Fresnel lens whose beacon can be seen from a distance of about eighteen miles. After 150 years and
two previous incarnations, this lighthouse remains
vital to navigation.

LEGENDARY LIGHTHOUSES

lighthouse keepers, such as John Tregembo, who was once an assistant keeper at the isolated Rock of Ages Lighthouse in Lake Superior. John returned to the lighthouse for the first time in fifty years with our television crew and a Coast Guard maintenance team.

You'll hear the stories of famous women light keepers such as Ida Lewis and Emily Fish. A series of heroic rescues in Rhode Island's Narragansett Bay made Ida a celebrity and a legend in her own time. Emily, the so-called "Social-Light Keeper," entertained lavishly while doing a very respectable job as keeper of the Point Pinos Lighthouse on the beautiful Monterey Peninsula.

You'll also meet Coast Guard Petty Officer Scott Stanton, America's last official lighthouse keeper. Stanton heads up a three-man crew at the still-functioning Boston Light Station on Little Brewster Island in Boston Harbor. Stanton and his crew are less isolated than earlier keepers who served here as long ago as 1716.

"I think it was a much harder job back then," says Stanton. "They had to row their boats everywhere they went. They couldn't just run ashore for food and water." Today, Little Brewster island remains a lonely place. Even so, Stanton describes his assignment as "the best job in the Coast Guard."

Some readers may be surprised to learn that, except at Boston, there are no more full-time government lighthouse keepers. Over the last few decades, new technologies have diminished the importance of lighthouses as aids to navigation, and the Coast Guard has automated one light station after another. Boston is now the only remaining officially manned U.S. light station.

Lindsay Smith

While the public would like to see the nation's lighthouse heritage preserved, tight budgets and a changing mission have put the Coast Guard in a tough position. Although it does an excellent job of maintaining and modernizing navigational lights and fog signals, the Coast Guard has little or no money for preserving historic structures. As a result, many old lighthouses have been left to decay and fall into ruin.

Fortunately, lighthouses have lots of

friends, and there are many people nowadays with a passionate interest in preserving them. The effort to save and restore endangered lighthouses takes place largely on a grass-roots level, but the Coast Guard does what it can to assist. In recent years it has transferred responsibility for and, in some cases, ownership of the lighthouses to private groups and government agencies.

Jim Walker is a lighthouse friend. A retired, thirty-year Coast Guard veteran, Jim heads up a group of volunteers now restoring the isolated Race Point Lighthouse on Cape Cod. It's a big job, and Walker and his volunteers take it one step at a time. "If you added up all the tanks of gas, phone calls, and odds and ends we have brought down here, the price would be prohibitive," says Walker. "But a little bit at a time doesn't seem to hurt so bad."

Why does he do it? "To spend the night here and watch the sunset," says Walker, "is worth an awful lot of work."

Lighthouses have been helping others for hundreds of years, but now they themselves need our assistance. In a variety of interesting and innovative ways, concerned local citizens are providing that help. They are, in a very real sense, the lighthouse keepers of today. And by reminding us of the need to preserve our heritage, lighthouses have become a new and perhaps even more important type of beacon.

Charlotte Johnson

Rose Island Light

"Rose Island Lighthouse is the object of all sorts of affection," says Charlotte Johnson. She led the effort to restore this tiny island light station in Rhode Island's Narragansett Bay and now looks after the lighthouse and the guests who stay there. At Rose Island visitors can actually live and work as keepers, if only for a few days. Guests not only have a good time, but they learn about the way ordinary folks, including lighthouse keepers, lived a century ago. They learn that it wasn't such an easy life—or such a bad one. And, perhaps, they learn a thing or two about their own lives and themselves.

Charlotte encourages the same type of experience at Rose Island that we hope you will have with this book and with the *Legendary Lighthouses* television series. As Charlotte says, "We invite people to go back in time as far as their imaginations can take them."

Have a nice trip.

Long

Gateway National
Recreation Area

New York

Lower Bay

Staten
Island

Sandy Hook Light

Sandy Hook

Navesink Lights

Concord Point Light

Turkey Point
Light

Havre de Grace

Baltimore

Seven Foot Knoll Light

Lightship Chesapeake

Atlantic City

Sandy Point Shoal Light

Dover

Annapolis

Thomas Point Light

Hooper Strait Light

St. Michaels

Easton

Cove Point Light

Solomons

Drum Point Light

Point No Point Light

Wolf Trap Light

Chesapeake Bay

Hampton

Old Point Comfort Light

Newport News

Old and New Cape Henry Lights

Norfolk

Virginia Beach

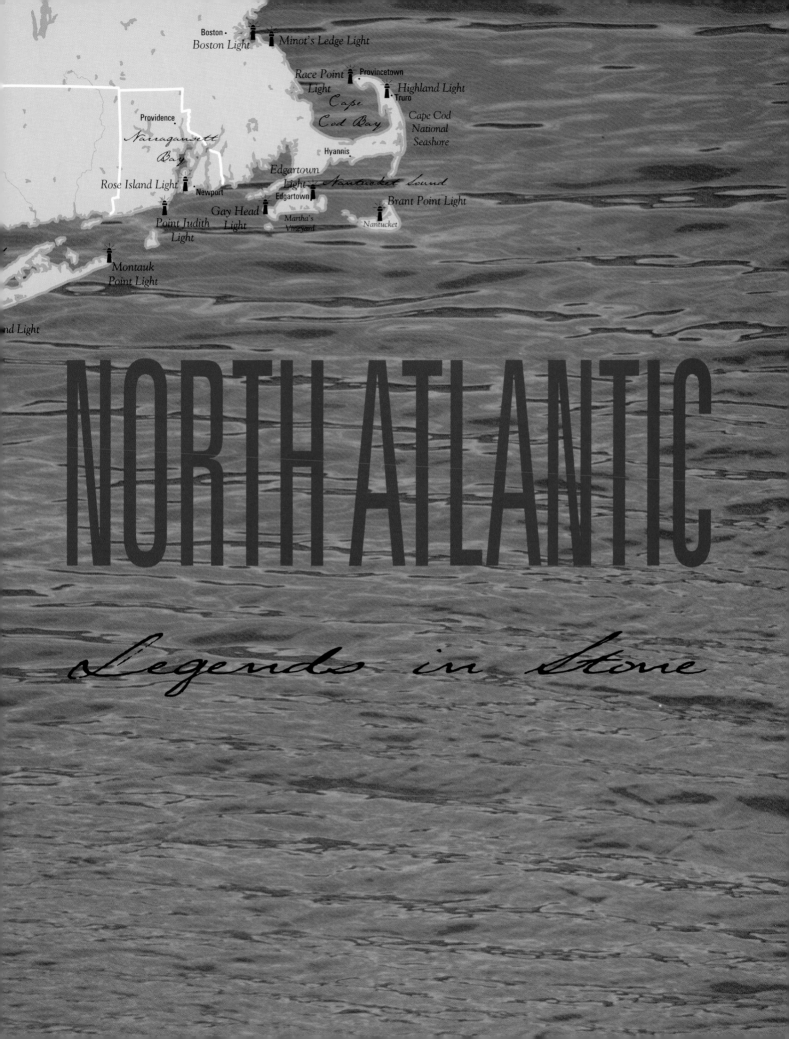

Boston ·
Boston Light   Minot's Ledge Light

Race Point   Provincetown
Light   Highland Light
Cape   Truro
Cod Bay   Cape Cod
National
Seashore
Hyannis

Providence ·
Narragansett
Bay   Edgartown
Light   *Nantucket Sound*
Rose Island Light   Edgartown   Brant Point Light
Newport
Gay Head   *Martha's*
Point Judith   Light   *Vineyard*   Nantucket
Light

Montauk
Point Light

nd Light

NORTH ATLANTIC

Legends in Stone

Legends in Stone

L ighthouses long ago made a pact with their old enemy, the night. In return for giving them a reason to exist and a black sky to brighten with their controlled lightning, these coastal sentinels gave darkness a home within their walls. At least that
is a legend held true by old-time lighthouse keepers, or wickies, who could never
find enough oil lamps to drive the shadows from their cavernous towers.

Even during the day, with the lights turned on, it seems dark inside the two-century-
old Boston Lighthouse. The interior of the eighty-nine-foot stone tower receives very little

Scott Stanton

sun, just a splash here and there
from a few tiny windows. Coast
Guard Petty Officer Scott Stanton
takes special care climbing the iron
staircase, which spirals upward
through permanent twilight.

When Stanton reaches the
top, however, an extraordinary
thing happens. The gloom surren-
ders to a flood of daylight pouring
in from all directions. Here, more
than ten stories above the ocean, a
large circular room opens onto a
360-degree panorama with the city
of Boston to the west and the shining Atlantic to the east. Usually, only seagulls get to enjoy
such a view, but for Stanton, it is a daily benefit of his employment.

Stanton's job is exceptional in more ways than one, since his profession stands on the
verge of extinction. During the last twenty years, the Coast Guard has automated the beacons and boarded up the dwellings of lighthouses along every U.S. coast. Now the only
remaining light station with a full-time crew is the one on Little Brewster Island at the outer
edge of Boston Harbor. In charge of a three-man Coast Guard team assigned here, Stanton
is, in effect, the last official lighthouse keeper in America.

The duties handled by Stanton and his team are not very different from those of thousands of other keepers who have served in the past at Little Brewster and hundreds of other
light stations guarding our coasts and lakeshores. "We start off with climbing the tower and
securing the light," says Stanton. "When we come down, we check the weather and pass that
information along to the Coast Guard group in Boston. Then we turn to our normal work
routine, which is basically maintenance, cleaning, and taking care of our boat and the structures on the island."

Boston Lighthouse stands guard over the rocks, grass, and flowers of Little
Brewster Island, just as it has since 1716. The nation's oldest navigational light
station, it has guided ships in and out of Boston Harbor for the better part of
three centuries. The tower seen here was built in 1783 to replace the original
one blown up by the British during the Revolutionary War.

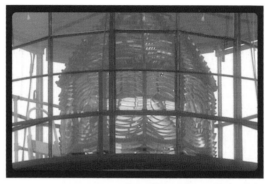

Fresnel lens at Boston Harbor Light

At the moment Stanton is checking the delicate lighting apparatus at the top of the tower. It is bright enough up here to make the keeper squint and cause a PBS film crew to adjust camera settings. The glare comes not just from beyond the ten-foot-high windows but from within as well. At the center of the room, almost filling it, are two tons of luminance. The station's enormous, second-order Fresnel lens appears to be sculpted in frozen light. Actually it is a matrix of several hundred highly polished glass prisms arrayed in a brass frame, but light is its business or, one might say, its art.

Manufactured in Paris, the big lens was shipped across the ocean and installed in this room in 1859, shortly before the Civil War. It was designed to gather every flicker from an oil lamp and focus the light into a beam so concentrated that it could be seen from the far horizon. Nowadays, the light is produced by an electric bulb rather than a burning wick, but the 140-year-old lens still does the hard part. Rotated by heavy machinery, it throws its flashing light more than two dozen miles out to sea.

"The lens gets a weekly cleaning with a lint-free cloth," says Stanton, giving several of the green-tinted prisms a quick inspection. "If there are hand marks or smudges, we take a little Windex to it." Dirty windows take on a whole new meaning when you work in a lighthouse. Stanton makes sure all the glass in the lantern room is cleaned inside and out at least twice a month. Also, the motor, gears, and metal wheels that keep the lens turning have to be oiled and greased regularly. There is plenty to do around the station. "There's always something that needs fixing," explains Stanton. "Always something that needs to be painted."

Stanton and the other young coastguardsmen who live and work here stay busy, and this helps them keep their minds off the isolation and the absence of friends and family who live across the water on the mainland. By comparison to many light stations, some of which can barely be reached at all, Boston Lighthouse is not very far from civilization. Point Allerton and the community of Hull are a couple of miles away by boat and only a little further is metropolitan Boston. Nonetheless, the distance to shore is a telling one. Going into town for food or supplies may take up to half a day, and even the simplest activities, such as turning on a tap, cannot be taken for granted on Little Brewster. The freshwater supply on the barren island is a constant concern.

Almost every day during the warm-weather months, boatloads of tourists come out to enjoy a water view of the old lighthouse. The tour boats never stop, but the passengers nearly always wave as they pass by the island. While there are occasionally visitors on the grounds, the station is officially closed to the public. Stanton admits that it does get lonely. "You just put that in the back of your head and try not to worry about it too much," he says.

To break the routine and maintain their contacts on the mainland, the members of the station team take shore leave on a rotating schedule, two weeks on the island and one week off. Two of them are always on duty. Theirs is a schedule and a type of work that most would not choose. "You either love it or you don't," declares Stanton. "The three of us happen to love it. We think we have the best jobs in the Coast Guard."

And as they go about their daily and nightly routines of maintaining the lighthouse, of keeping its beacon shining and its fog signal sounding, the team on Little Brewster continues a tradition that reaches back more than 280 years. With a few intervals, such as when the British blew up the original tower during the American Revolution, there has been a keeper on duty here continuously since 1716.

A very old and remarkable roster kept in a small room below the tower contains the names of all sixty-six Boston Lighthouse keepers and their terms of service. Some lived on Little Brewster for only a year or two. Others, such as George Ball, who served here from 1733 until 1774, kept the light for decades. Likely, Scott Stanton will only be here for a few years, but when he is eventually assigned to other duties, his name will be added to the role.

"It's quite amazing to picture my name on that list," he says. "It's a thrill to carry on the tradition of all the Lighthouse Service and Coast Guard keepers who have been here before me. I don't think I'm going to get the full impact of it all until I leave here and look back and say, 'Wow, that was a pretty neat job.'"

A Bell for the Keepers

At the top of the list of sixty-six Boston Light keepers is the name George Worthylake and beside it the dates 1716 to 1718. Whereas Stanton is America's last lighthouse keeper, Worthylake was its first. Having built a stone tower on Little Brewster Island to attract commerce to their city, the merchants of Boston offered Worthylake fifty British pounds a year to keep its tallow candles burning. A harbor pilot and shepherd with a large family, he was glad enough of the money and the job. In the end, however, the work proved far less financially rewarding than he had hoped.

Worthylake's responsibilities as keeper proved so arduous and time-consuming that he had little time left over for piloting ships into the harbor. Even worse, a horrendous gale swept over the island and drowned his herd of fifty-nine sheep, leaving Worthylake practically penniless. He pleaded with his employers for assistance. The town of Boston granted him an increase of twenty pounds in his annual salary, but the unlucky keeper never got to spend the money. On his way back from Boston, where he had gone to collect his pay, Worthylake's open boat capsized only a hundred yards or so from the dock on Little Brewster Island. Swimming in the icy waters was impossible and the keeper soon slipped beneath the waves. Later, Worthylake's body washed up on the same low sand spit where his sheep had perished.

Minots Ledge Lighthouse marks a dangerous open-water shoal just off Cohasset, Massachusetts. The granite structure shown here replaced an iron-skeleton tower destroyed by a storm in 1851.

A man named Robert Saunders replaced the unfortunate Worthylake. Saunders had barely settled into the keeper's residence on Little Brewster when he, too, drowned in a boating accident. The profession of lighthouse keeping had gotten off to an inauspicious beginning in America. But it would continue, for the work done by keepers was vitally necessary.

Over the centuries since George Worthylake lit the first candle in the lantern room atop the Little Brewster tower, lighthouses and their keepers have guided a steady stream of merchant ships to American harbors, guaranteeing the prosperity of port cities such as Boston, New York, Baltimore, and San Francisco. They have warned countless vessels away from ship-killing obstacles such as Diamond Shoals off Cape Hatteras, the Rock of Ages in Lake Superior, St. George's Reef off the northern California coast, or Graves Ledge just north of Little Brewster Island. And fortunately for all concerned, the personal stories of most keepers have ended far more happily than those of Worthylake and Saunders. Otherwise, who would have kept the lights?

But lighthouse keeping has always been hazardous work. Its dangers were never more dramatically illustrated than in the tragedy that struck the Minots Ledge Light Station in 1851. Only a few miles southeast of the Boston Lighthouse, a vicious shoal lurks just beneath the surface waiting to tear open the hulls of unwary ships. For many years, building a lighthouse on the rock known as Minots Ledge was thought impossible. Mariners sailing the waters off Cohasset were forced to rely on dead reckoning and good fortune to avert disaster. Naturally, not all these navigators were lucky, and the shoal exacted a ghastly toll of barks, brigs, coasters, ketches, schooners, and large ships, along with many passengers and crews.

Then, in 1847, a young engineer named I.W.P. Lewis put forward his radical plan for a lighthouse to be built in open water directly over the ledge. Instead of the usual stone cylinder, the tower would consist of an iron skeleton much like those later built on reefs in the Florida Keys. The tower, lantern, and keeper's dwelling would stand on iron legs anchored to pilings driven deep into the subsurface rock. In theory at least, the spidery structure would offer little resistance to wind and water and even the most formidable waves would pass harmlessly through it.

Completed at enormous cost over a period of nearly three years, the experimental lighthouse entered service on New Year's Day in 1850. Initially, all went well, and mariners were glad of the beacon, which helped them keep their distance from the deadly ledge. But almost from the first the keepers—a team of three like the one now stationed at the Boston Lighthouse—noticed a queasy swaying motion when storms hit the tower.

Keeper John Bennett happened to be ashore on leave when an especially powerful gale struck the area on the night of March 16–17, 1851. He had left the station in the hands of his assistants, Joseph Wilson and Joseph Antoine, and as the fury of storm increased, Bennett grew increasingly concerned for their safety. His fears proved well founded. Pounded repeatedly by huge waves welling up off the sea bottom, the skeleton tower leaned over and finally collapsed into the ocean. The grief-stricken Bennett noted with pride that his assistants had kept the light burning almost to the last instant. He would always remember the station bell ringing out wildly as the waves swept over the tower.

It took the Lighthouse Service years to look past the loss it suffered at Cohasset, but the

Ocean rollers pound New England's **Minots Ledge Lighthouse** tower. Built with massive granite blocks that throw waves harmlessly aside, it has stood up to the sea for more than 135 years.

fallen Minots Ledge Lighthouse was eventually replaced. Completed in 1860, the new tower was made of stone rather than iron. Its massive granite blocks were assembled in such a way that the pressure of storm-driven waves causes them to grip one another ever more tightly. The ninety-seven-foot tower actually gets stronger in a gale. For nearly a century keepers lived within its massive walls with little fear of being swept off the rock. Automated in 1947, the lighthouse now stands alone, but still does its job as faithfully as ever.

The Many Keepers of Rose Island Light

With the single exception of the Boston Light Station, where a full-time crew is maintained for historical reasons, the automation of America's lighthouses is now complete. Electric timers or radio-activated switches turn on and off the lights and fog signals, while mechanical sensors alert centralized Coast Guard monitoring stations when bulbs blow out or something needs fixing. In many cases solar cells provide power for the lights. Since there are no resident keepers, no one needs to face dangers like those that took the lives of Worthylake, Saunders, Antoine, Wilson, and so many others over the years.

Ironically, the lighthouses themselves are now the ones in danger. They are threatened not so much by storms or accidents but by the ravages of time and neglect. In recent years radar and satellite direction finding have made pinpoint navigation possible, and the lights are no longer as important as they once were to mariners. Budget cutbacks have left the Coast Guard little money for unnecessary spending, and as a result, automated or discontinued lighthouses have been allowed to fall into ruin. In some cases the deterioration is irreparable and the old towers and dwellings are torn down. Increasingly aware of their symbolic and historical value, however, the public is demanding that endangered lighthouses be saved. In fact, lighthouses may be more popular now than ever before.

According to Charlotte Johnson, she has never met anyone who "didn't like a lighthouse or a caboose." Johnson is executive director of the Rose Island Lighthouse Foundation in Rhode Island, and as such, she is an example of an entirely new variety of lighthouse keeper. Old-time keepers lived full-time at their station, operated its light and fog signal, polished its lens, oiled its machinery, repaired its equipment, painted its walls, reported on its weather, and sometimes rescued shipwrecked seamen. Although she may have done some of these things on occasion, Johnson sees her duties in a very different light. She has dedicated herself to rescuing a lighthouse from what would have been almost certain destruction.

Charlotte Johnson

"Rose Island Lighthouse is the object of all sorts of affection," says Johnson, who considers all lighthouses to be "generic symbols of people caring about other people." This particular lighthouse is an example of people caring about their heritage.

John Philip Hagen

Now a private aid to navigation, Rhode Island's **Rose Island Lighthouse** stands guard over the waters of Narragansett Bay. Abandoned by the Coast Guard during the 1970s, the structure has been lovingly restored by a local organization.

Located on a postage stamp of rock and soil in Rhode Island's Narragansett Bay, the Rose Island Lighthouse could hardly be less like the grand stone tower on Little Brewster Island and the other massive sentinels that guard our nation's outer coasts. Built in 1869, it is a wood-frame structure with a squarish thirty-five-foot tower rising through its mansard roof. Its architecture hints at French Empire and Victorian influence. The Rose Island beacon was never intended to signal ships far out to sea. Instead, it was meant to warn ships away from the island and guide them into the channel leading to industrious Providence.

The little lighthouse served its purpose well for just over a century. Then with the completion of the Newport Bridge, the Coast Guard closed the station in 1971. Rose Island's humble beacon was thought no longer necessary since the lofty red light on the bridge provided a far more effective navigational marker.

Over the next thirteen years, the abandoned lighthouse stood empty, while wind and rain invaded its walls and roof. Repeatedly scarred by vandals, it became an eyesore, and there was talk of bringing in a wrecking crew. Instead of wreckers, however, a preservation-minded group of local citizens took charge of the deteriorating lighthouse, which had been declared surplus property by the government. Calling themselves the Rose Island Lighthouse Foundation, they started raising money to refurbish the landmark. The effort took years, but by 1993 the foundation was able not only to restore the dwelling and tower but also to reestablish the light as a private aid to navigation.

Having returned to active service, the lighthouse performs its old function and a completely new one as well. People are allowed to stay here in the rooms that once housed the keepers and their families. Rentals go toward paying the cost of maintenance.

Often Johnson takes guests to the island herself. They bring their own food with them, and their expectations vary widely, for this is no ordinary inn. Those who come here are in for an adventure. Guest quarters are appointed much as they might have been early in the century when this was a Lighthouse Service duty station. There are brass beds with patchwork quilts, candles, coals stoves, and even wooden coffee grinders. Water must be hand pumped, and electric power, provided by wind generators, is unreliable at best and often altogether unavailable.

"We invite people to go back in time as far as their imaginations can take them," says Johnson. Most visitors get far enough to learn more than a little about how keepers and other ordinary Americans lived at the turn of the twentieth century.

However, the extraordinary quality of the Rose Island experience goes beyond the antique atmosphere of the place. What makes it unique is the fact that guests are assigned duties. Whether they stay for a week or just overnight, they become, in effect, keepers of the Rose Island Lighthouse. The light itself operates automatically and requires little care, but other chores, such as raising the flag, recording weather readings, and adding chlorine to the water supply, must be completed. As an additional duty, keepers greet curious day-visitors who come by private boat for a look at the old lighthouse.

"The first time keepers come out here, I think they're pretty overwhelmed with the responsibilities," says Johnson. "But it gets ironed out. Everybody takes care of themselves and the lighthouse. The neatest thing is seeing how satisfied people are with themselves when they leave."

Heroine of Lime Rock

Rose Island Lighthouse was a familiar site to a remarkable woman who became a legend in her own time and America's most renowned lighthouse keeper. She earned her fame with daring rescues of drowning children, seaman, and even farm animals from the cold waters of Rhode Island's Narragansett Bay. In time she would be so well-known that writers, tycoons, and presidents clamored to visit her.

Just across the bay from Rose Island is the Ida Lewis Yacht Club, which occupies the living quarters of the old Lime Rock Lighthouse. The club is named for the daughter of an ailing sea captain and revenue cutter pilot who served for many years as keeper of the light. A modest light station, nothing more than a harbor marker really, Lime Rock was nevertheless home to one of the most famous women of the nineteenth century.

Born in 1842, Ida Lewis grew up in what was known as "straightened circumstances." Her father's illness made it impossible for him to provide his family with more than the small sum he was paid for keeping the Lime Rock Light. In time even these duties proved too much for him, and the teenaged Ida was forced to take over the care and cleaning of the station's tiny lamp and lens. Meanwhile she also helped raise her brother and younger sisters. But her heavy load of family responsibilities never prevented Ida from helping a stranger in need.

Ida was strong limbed and could handle a boat, qualities she put to good use whenever some hapless person fell overboard in Newport's harbor. Should anyone need assistance, she would hop into the station skiff and pull hard on the oars until she reached their side. Usually, she simply grabbed them by the coat or shirt collar and yanked them over into the boat. By the age of sixteen, Ida had rescued at least four people and perhaps more. Her exploits continued as she finished her schooling and grew into a young woman.

Courtesy of U.S. Coast Guard

Ida Lewis's daring rescues made her one of America's best known lighthouse keepers.

Courtesy of U.S. Coast Guard

Lime Rock in Ida Lewis's time.

"Ida did things that women usually didn't do in her day," says Elinor deWire, author of *Guardians of the Light*, a book about keepers. "She pulled up her skirts, got into a boat, and rowed to the rescue."

In 1867 Ida pulled three men and a prized sheep from the Narragansett. Then, two years later, came the incident that would put her name in newspapers and magazines across the country. During a stiff March gale, high waves overturned a boat filled with soldiers from a nearby fort. Although suffering from a severe respiratory ailment, Ida ignored her mother's protests and rushed off to the rescue. She reached the capsized boat just in time to save the numb and exhausted soldiers. This dramatic story ended up in the *New York Times* and *Leslie's Magazine* and put Ida Lewis on the cover of the most widely circulated publication of the era, *Harpers Weekly*.

"This caught on with the press and they made a big deal out of it," says deWire. "People fell in love with the idea that here was this young girl doing all these self-sacrificing things and making a good name for the ladies."

At one time or another, the Vanderbilts, the Belmonts, the Astors, and many other notables came here to have tea with Ida Lewis. The Lime Rock guest book must have made for interesting reading.

Unlike today's media darlings, however, Ida never cashed in on her celebrity. Instead, when Captain Lewis died in 1872, she took over as keeper of the Lime Rock Light. For nearly forty years afterward, she faithfully tended the light. On the night she died in 1911, the bells of vessels anchored in Newport Harbor rang until dawn.

Elinor deWire

Back from the Brink

Although they never became famous as Ida Lewis did, the light keepers of Cape Cod often rushed to the rescue of drowning mariners. With its great sweeping arm extending more than seventy miles out into the Atlantic, the Cape is one of the most formidable navigational obstacles on the planet. Over the centuries, more than three thousand vessels have come to grief on the Cape's coarse glacial sands. No one knows how many seamen have perished on the Cape or how many others were rescued by the keepers and lifesavers stationed here.

Fishermen off Cape Cod

The same things that make the Cape so dangerous to ships—its marriage to the ocean and its shifting sands—have also made it a tourist mecca. Cape Cod National Seashore offers 44,600 acres of protected cranberry bogs and beaches where majestic dunes may pile up to a height of one hundred feet or more. Visitors will find villages here where New England's early maritime culture lives on and dirt roads little changed since Henry David Thoreau walked them 150 years ago. And at night, almost anywhere they look, they will see the flash of navigational beacons.

Because of its threat to shipping, Cape Cod is a place of many lighthouses. In all, seventeen were built over a period of about a century. Today, seven working light stations remain along with remnants of several others. Taken together, these represent one of the finest accessible collections of coastal lighthouses in the world. And for many travelers, they are an essential part of the Cape Cod experience.

"A lot of people who come down here are looking for a warm and friendly beacon," says Greg O'Brien. An author and producer of films about the Cape, O'Brien has spent much of his life here. For him, Cape Cod itself has been a guiding beacon. "It's not only the beauty," he says. "It's the sound, the smell, the light. Every day the sea is carving up the

Greg O'Brien

21

Established in 1798, the **Cape Cod (Highland) Lighthouse** was rebuilt in 1857. Recently, it was moved to keep it from falling over the Cape's rapidly eroding cliffs.

shoreline, and you can go down to Truro or Provincetown or Wellfleet and see a different beach every day."

Like nearly everyone who treasures the Cape, O'Brien is a fan of lighthouses, and the one at Truro is perhaps his favorite. The Highland Light, established in 1797, was Cape Cod's first major navigational beacon. During the mid-1850s, the original lighthouse had to be rebuilt when the land beneath it crumbled into the sea. Only recently, the sixty-six-foot brick tower that replaced it faced the same unhappy destiny.

"The ocean has eaten away steadily at Cape Cod," says O'Brien. "The Highland Light was getting very close to the edge of the bluff—within about fifty feet of going over."

By the 1990s the Highland Station, known to most nowadays as the Cape Cod Lighthouse, teetered precariously atop a rapidly eroding cliff of compressed sand. People could actually watch large pieces of the bank break away and tumble down. It became obvious to one and all that unless something was done soon, the lighthouse would end up in a jumbled heap on the beach.

At this point the Truro Historical Society brought in engineers to see what could be done to save the lighthouse. The solution turned out to be quite simple, though technically challenging and expensive: The lighthouse had to be moved. Cost estimates for moving the tower and other structures back to a safe distance of about five hundred feet from the cliffs ranged upward to as much as $1.5 million. Undeterred by the hefty price tag, the society sought financial assistance from the Commonwealth of Massachusetts, the National Park Service, the Coast Guard, the town of Truro, and even a local golf course. By 1996 the necessary funds had been raised, and the project got under way.

"It was incredible to watch," says O'Brien, who described the relocation process as "a combination of high-tech and common horse sense." To prevent the 140-year-old brick tower from falling apart during the move, a concrete compression ring was formed within its walls. A jacket of steel protected the exterior. Supported by steel beams, the tower was then lifted by hydraulic jacks and pushed along over heavy rollers at a pace so painstakingly slow that the crowds who came to watch could not see it move. Finally, however, the tower reached its new home. "It's safe for now," says O'Brien. "If my family stays here on the Cape, generations from now maybe my descendants will be involved in the next move."

If the lighthouse is threatened again, O'Brien feels sure the people here will do whatever is necessary to save it. "The lighthouse is a connection to the past," he says. "If you lose the past, you lose Cape Cod."

One Can of Paint at a Time

Most lighthouse restoration projects are not major government or community undertakings. At Race Point, about ten miles northeast of Truro, Jim Walker and a few friends wage a lonely battle to defend one of Cape Cod's links to the past. A veteran of thirty years in the Coast Guard, Walker heads a small group of volunteers struggling to restore the Race Point Lighthouse.

"This is the one that was forgotten," Walker says of the modest light station, established during the nineteenth century to guide vessels around the tip of Cape Cod. "This is the one that everybody walked away from. It just sat here for twenty years."

The cast-iron tower and wooden dwelling are located on one of the most isolated stretches of the Cape, a place known for fierce, unpredictable currents and numerous shipwrecks. It is called the Race.

"The Race itself is a very strange place," says Walker. "There are miles and miles of nothing but dunes and beach, and the sand is so soft that walking on it is very tiring."

Practically inaccessible, the Race Point Lighthouse was never a choice duty station for keepers. Nor was it well regarded by mariners. The station dates to 1816 when a rubblestone tower

Jim Walker

Race Point Light

was erected on the yielding sands of the point. Equipped with primitive spider lamps, the lighthouse did little to slow the pace of wrecks in the turbulent waters of the Race. A lamp-and-reflector system installed by Winslow Lewis—a New England sea captain turned inventor and lighthouse contractor—barely improved the situation. A fourth-order Fresnel lens put in place after the existing iron tower was built in 1876 made the light more effective, but the remote station was always difficult to maintain and supply. Finally, in 1978 the Coast Guard automated the beacon and more or less gave up on the lighthouse.

"I believe the Coast Guard intended to tear it down if somebody didn't come along to do something with it—and fairly quickly," says Walker.

Somebody did. In 1995 the New England Lighthouse Foundation leased the property, and Walker set to work. What he and his volunteers found here would have been enough to discourage all but the most determined lighthouse preservationists. The walls of the dwelling were rotten, and the tower was streaked with rust. In short, the place was a mess.

"Somebody had stolen all the electrical wiring," says Walker. "The panels and light fixtures were all missing. It was a nightmare trying to put it all back together again."

Indeed, the restoration is still a long way from complete. It may go on for years, with each new task handled as time and money become available. "If we added up all the tanks of gas, phone calls, and odds and ends we have brought down here, the price would be prohibitive," Walker says with a shake of his head. "But a little bit at a time doesn't seem to hurt so bad."

Like other lighthouse friends, each of whom nurture their own special motives, Walker has no trouble at all explaining why he has taken on this project. "To spend the night here and watch the sunset is worth an awful lot of work."

Whales and Prisms

The natural beauty that rewards Jim Walker for his hard work at the Race Point Lighthouse has made much of southern New England a magnet for tourists. While many summer travelers flock to Cape Cod, others choose to take their coastal adventures even farther from the mainland of their day-to-day lives by boarding crowded ferries bound for Martha's Vineyard or Nantucket.

Although separated from the Cape by miles of open water, these sizable islands have much in common with it. They were created by the same geological forces—the glaciers that, up until ten thousand years ago, blanketed much of the continent and dumped masses of gravel and sand into the Atlantic. Thanks to the coarse glacial sands, Cape Cod, Martha's Vineyard, and Nantucket can boast some of the loveliest beaches in America. But they also share a human bond. All three were important outposts of New England's traditional fishing, whaling, and sea-trading culture.

On Martha's Vineyard, traces of this rich maritime heritage can be seen everywhere, for instance, in the magnificent Whaling Church and stately sea captain's homes of Edgartown. Especially evocative of the past are the five navigational lights that still guide mariners through the treacherous seas surrounding the boat-shaped island. The oldest and best known of them is the Gay Head Lighthouse, which takes its name from the streaks of bright color decorating the mineral-laden cliffs below the station.

The Victorian-style brick, brownstone, and steel tower seen on Gay Head today dates to before the Civil War. When the tower was completed in 1856, its lantern room was fitted with the best and most powerful optic available at the time: a first-order Fresnel lens.

Edgartown Whaling Church

"The Fresnel lens was an engineering marvel," says Bruce Andrews, director of the Dukes County Historical Society. "This one was at Gay Head from 1856 to 1952, so it sure served its purpose." After almost a century of service, the huge lens was replaced by an automated beacon similar to those used at airports. Since the new, automated light required little maintenance, the station's keepers were reassigned. Its residences and

Gay Head Light

Bruce Andrews

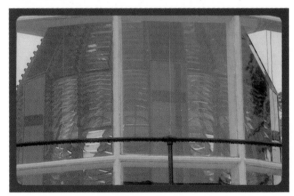

Gay Head Fresnel

other support buildings were demolished, and only the tower was left standing.

"Gay Head was one of the last areas on Martha's Vineyard to get electricity," says Andrews. "When it did, they decided the Fresnel wasn't necessary anymore." At the time the lens was removed by the Coast Guard during the early 1950s, the U.S. government and the American public placed far more value on function than on the historical qualities of buildings and equipment. Supposedly outmoded devices such as nineteenth-century lighthouse lenses were often regarded as little more than useless junk.

"Their first thought was to mash it up and bury it so they wouldn't have to worry about it," says Andrews.

Fortunately, the Gay Head lens was saved by the tradition-minded residents of Martha's Vineyard. Today, the lens is on display at the Historical Society Museum in Edgartown. This museum is a good place (as is the Montauk Point Museum mentioned in the next section) to learn about the prismatic lenses invented by French engineer Augustine Fresnel in 1822.

Fresnel's highly polished glass optics revolutionized lighthouse technology by making navigational beacons much more powerful and reliable. The increased power led to the construction of taller towers on outer coasts facing the open ocean—now their beacons could reach far out over the horizon. And the improved reliability meant that even small harbors could be marked effectively with lights.

Fresnel lenses varied in size according to the focusing power required of them and were designated first-order, second-order, and so on, down through sixth-order. Nearly twelve feet tall and with an interior diameter of more than six feet, the first-order lenses were by far the largest and most powerful—a few even bigger "hyper-radial" lenses were made. The smallest were the diminutive sixth-order lenses, about the size of an ordinary table lamp. The larger first-, second-, and third-order lenses were used along the coast, while the smaller-order lenses marked river channels and harbors.

Until recently, the Edgartown Lighthouse on the western edge of the inner harbor just across from Chappaquiddick Island employed a medium-sized fourth-order lens. Today, its guiding light is produced by a small acrylic lens. Plastic lenses such as this one are no more powerful or effective than the antique Fresnel lenses they replaced. They are, however, much easier to automate and maintain, which explains the Coast Guard's preference for them.

Surrounded by the blue waters of Long Island Sound, the **New London Ledge Lighthouse** appears dramatically out of place. Built in 1909, the light was automated by the Coast Guard in 1987. Since then the building has stood empty—except for "Ernie," the ghost said to haunt the tower.

A fifth-order Fresnel lens still shines in the notably historic Brant Point Lighthouse on Nantucket. No ferry enters the harbor at Nantucket without passing the squat structure, but most passengers are likely unaware of the station's remarkable past. This is America's second-oldest light—the Boston Light was established about thirty years earlier.

In 1746, tired of seeing their whaling ships miss the harbor and wreck on nearby beaches, Nantucket residents voted an outlay of 200 British pounds to pay for construction of a wooden lighthouse on Brant Point. Today, more than 250 years later, a light tower still stands on the point, but it is not the original. A dozen years after it was completed, the first tower burned to the ground. This was never a lucky lighthouse, and later towers also burned or were undercut by erosion, bowled over by high winds, washed out to sea by the tides, or eaten up by rot. Since its beacon was much needed, the little lighthouse was always rebuilt, and over the years, ten separate light towers marked Brant Point.

The existing tower, built in 1901, has survived for almost a century. Little more than twenty feet tall, it is one of the shortest lighthouses in America—and is certainly the one most frequently rebuilt. But its small size does nothing to diminish its value for the people of Nantucket, who see in it a reminder of the days, now long past, when their town was among the world's busiest whaling ports, or for the masters of vessels who still follow its red light into the harbor. Tourists also have a special affection for the light, which provides a welcome and farewell as they come and go on ferries. According to legend, throwing two pennies overboard as you round the lighthouse will ensure a safe crossing.

Brandt Point

A Lamp at the Door

Ships arriving off our shores after an Atlantic crossing are often greeted by the bright flash of a beacon shining from Montauk Point at the far eastern end of Long Island. This light has provided generations of immigrants with their first glimpse of America. It is easy to imagine them crowding the rails of passenger liners and straining their eyes to catch sight of it. At night, they could see the Montauk Point beacon long before detecting any other evidence of land. During the day, if their ship came close enough, they might enjoy a view of the lighthouse itself. For many, its majestic tower was a symbol of the freedom and opportunity waiting for them in their new country.

Some think of the Montauk Point Light as no less a national icon than the Statue of Liberty, which also served for many years as a navigational light. Certainly it is a venerable structure and is, in fact, much older than Lady Liberty. Built during the administration of President George Washington, it was completed in 1796.

Even before its official beacon went into service more than two centuries ago, in 1796, Montauk Point was, on occasion, marked by lights. Long ago, Indian tribes built signal pyres on Montauk's Turtle Hill to guide their war canoes across Long Island Sound. During the Revolutionary War, British naval forces placed a temporary light here to help their fighting ships avoid the shoals just off the point.

Whales sometimes get trapped in the shallows off Montauk, and they nearly always perish before the tides can release them. Over the years, the Montauk Light has earned the friendship of countless seamen by saving their ships from a similar fate. Nowadays, however, the lighthouse may be even more popular with landlubbers than it is with mariners. During its early years, the Montauk Station attracted only the most adventurous travelers who might stop by to share a mug of hot coffee with the keeper. Today, it ranks among America's most visited lighthouses. People flock to Montauk to explore the excellent museum located in the rambling nineteenth-century keeper's residence and to enjoy the splendid natural setting.

Dick White

"Gorgeous, absolutely gorgeous," Dick White says of the old light station. As president of the Montauk Lighthouse Foundation, White gets to spend a lot of time here. "I was born and raised in Montauk, and the lighthouse has been part of my life for more than half a century. It's just very special, very impressive up on top of the hill with its white and brown stripes, the green all around, and water on two sides."

The octagonal tower of **Montauk Lighthouse** rises over the station's old keeper's dwelling, now a fascinating maritime museum. Established in 1797, the Montauk Light marks the far eastern end of New York's Long Island.

The eighty-foot-tall Montauk bluffs offer an expansive view. In clear weather sharp-eyed visitors can see Point Judith, Rhode Island, more than twenty miles to the north. "And if you are really tall you can see all the way to Portugal," White says with a wink.

White was among the local preservationists who rallied to save the residence and other historic station buildings after the Coast Guard automated the light and removed the full-time crew in 1987. Usually, when lights are automated, the dwellings and other unnecessary structures are demolished or allowed to deteriorate. To keep this from happening at Montauk, the Montauk Lighthouse Foundation refurbished the large keeper's duplex for use as a museum.

Montauk Point Lighthouse Museum

Featuring a fine collection of lighthouse lamps and lenses, the museum draws a steady stream of tourists, especially during the summer. "It gets over 100,000 visitors a year," says White.

Among the displays is the unusual, clam-shaped lens employed at Montauk from 1904 until the automation in 1987. Slightly smaller than a standard third-order Fresnel, this revolving "bivalve" lens once focused a flashing beacon that could be seen from nineteen miles away. Interestingly, electric power was late in arriving at Montauk, and a kerosene lamp mounted inside the lens remained in use all the way up until 1938, when the Coast Guard installed a thousand-watt bulb.

Today, the lens still shines, its light playing eerily over the faces of museum visitors. "We can only put a forty-watt bulb in the lens," says White. "Otherwise we'd blind people."

Of particular interest to children is the museum's interactive diorama, as it allows them to become lighthouse keepers on a rather grand scale. Scattered across a colorful, three-dimensional map representing a two-hundred-mile stretch of the mid-Atlantic coast are dozens of Lilliputian light towers. With the push of a button, kids can bring to life the beacons of the Sandy Hook tower in northern New Jersey, the Beavertail tower just south of Newport, Rhode Island, and many others. A favorite button is the one that lights up a tiny replica of the Fire Island tower near the center of the diorama.

The real Fire Island Lighthouse, located about eighty miles west of Montauk, is no miniature. Soaring almost 170 feet above the island sands, it can be seen from the decks of ships long before they come within sight of land. At night the flashing Fire Island beacon is visible from up to twenty-four miles at sea. This light, like the one at Montauk, has provided more than a few passengers on trans-Atlantic liners with a bright welcome to America.

Ironically, Fire Island is not much like the rest of America. A narrow barrier of beaches and dunes guarding the south-central shore of Long Island, it is mostly wild, and nearly all of the island is included in a protected National Seashore. There are no shopping malls, filling stations, or swank restaurants here, and the daily experiences of residents and visitors are a world apart from those of New York City suburbanites who live only a few dozen miles away.

"Fire Island is different," says seashore ranger Dave Griese. "It's unique."

None of the seventeen small communities on the island allows cars. Groceries and other supplies arrive from the mainland by ferry and are carted home in vehicles that look very much like childhood wagons. In fact, that is exactly what they are—Radio Flyers and the like. "Those little red wagons provide people with a way to get their food and so forth to their homes," says Griese.

Fire Island Light

People and wildlife mingle freely on the island. Deer wander through yards at will and, when no one is looking, eat the flowers. Residents and visitors agree that time seems to stand still here, but Fire Island itself is constantly on the move. As with most other barrier islands along the Atlantic coast, the sands of Fire Island are steadily shifting—in this case toward the southwest at a rate of two hundred feet or more per year. When the current tower was completed a few years before the Civil War, it stood at the extreme western tip of the island.

Dave Griese

"Not anymore," says Griese.

Today, the island extends another six miles to the west. Presumably, in another thousand years or so, Fire Island will reach all the way to the mouth of the Hudson River.

A dock on Fire Island

Guards at the Gate

The Lower New York Bay has long been known to mariners as the gateway to the Hudson and the port of New York. To millions of immigrants who passed through it on the third-class decks of passenger liners, the bay was the gateway to America itself. But since the Lower Bay was pinched in by the long fingers of Rockaway Point to the north and Sandy Hook to the south, the gate has never been

Sandy Hook Light

wide open, and ships have trouble finding the entrance. For more than 230 years, they have had help. Since 1764, a dozen years before the signing of the Declaration of Independence, a navigational beacon shining from the bay's southern lip has pointed the way.

Nowadays, approximately 26,000 acres of beaches and wetlands surrounding the Lower Bay are gathered into the Gateway National Recreation Area. Managed by the National Park Service, the Gateway protects some of the East's most endangered wild lands—and one very old lighthouse.

During the early 1760s, in order to attract even more sea trade to their already bustling harbor, New York City merchants funded the construction of the Sandy Hook Lighthouse. There were four other light stations in America at that time: Little Brewster in Boston Harbor, Brant Point on Nantucket, Beavertail in Rhode Island, and New London in Connecticut. All four of these lighthouses were eventually destroyed or rebuilt, and none of them look the way they did during the pre-Revolutionary era. Remarkably, the original eight-sided rubblestone tower built by colonial masons on Sandy Hook still stands. What visitors will see here is nothing less than the oldest lighthouse in the United States.

Not surprising, the Sandy Hook station has an involved history. During the Revolutionary War, British and Continental forces fought several sharp skirmishes for possession of the strategic Sandy Hook peninsula and its lighthouse. With the help of their powerful navy, the British held the station for much of the war, but the Americans managed to destroy enough of its equipment to make the lighthouse of little use to the redcoats.

Later the Sandy Hook Lighthouse became the focus of a protracted legal war. Although located in New Jersey, the station was initially known as the New York Lighthouse and was, in fact, owned and operated by New Yorkers. The people of New Jersey felt the lighthouse should belong to them, however, and for many years the two states fought in and out of court over possession of the station. Finally, in 1790, the U.S. government put an end to the almost comical squabbling by taking federal control of the facility.

Sandy Hook visitors may be reminded of all this history each evening when the station lights up its 1857 third-order Fresnel lens. In use here for more than 140 years, the antique lens projects its fixed white beacon more than nineteen miles out to sea. Now automated, the old lens works about as well as any so-called modern optical device.

A few miles south of Sandy Hook and just outside the boundaries of the Gateway Recreation Area, a pair of stone light towers guards a prominent bluff overlooking the approaches to the Lower Bay. Although not nearly as old as the tower at Sandy Hook, they are of considerable historical note. Known as the Twin Lights of Navesink, or more commonly, the Highlands Lighthouse, they are open to the public as part of a historical site and museum operated by the state of New Jersey.

Thomas Laverty and bivalve lens frame

"The Highlands are a natural land formation that sticks up about two-hundred feet above sea level," says Thomas Laverty, a historic preservation specialist. "First noticed back in 1609 when Henry Hudson sailed into the area, the Highlands became a very distinctive navigational mark for sea captains entering the New York Harbor. It's a very narrow, shallow, and treacherous approach, so they need to know exactly where they are and make very precise movements."

Federal maritime authorities understood the importance of the Highlands, and in 1828 they built a lighthouse on the bluffs. To help mariners recognize the Navesink

The Twin Lights of Navesink

Light, the new station was given two separate towers spaced about a hundred yards apart. One tower had a fixed light and the other a flashing light. It was essential that mariners be able to distinguish the Navesink beacon from that of the Sandy Hook Light a short distance to the north.

"To get into the New York shipping channels, you had to go around the tip of Sandy Hook and past the Sandy Hook Lighthouse," says Laverty. "If you made a mistake and aimed for this lighthouse instead, you would end up sailing right onto the beach—with disastrous results."

The Navesink Lights were considered so vital to maritime commerce that the nation's first Fresnel lenses were installed in the two towers in 1841. This early experiment with the French-made prismatic lenses proved successful, and in time nearly every lighthouse in

State of New Jersey Division of Parks and Forestry

The octagonal brownstone structure above is the northernmost of two towers at **New Jersey's Highlands (Navesink) Lighthouse.** Now part of a popular maritime museum, the twin-towered light station was once among America's most important navigational markers—it pointed the way to New York. For many years this north tower held a first-order Fresnel lens of extraordinary power.

America would use them to focus their beacons and guide mariners. The Navesink Museum celebrates the crucial role this station played in the history of navigational technology with an extraordinary collection of lighthouse artifacts. One of these is an enormous first-order bivalve lens that once shined in the Navesink south tower.

"It's a very big light," says Laverty. "Nine and a half feet in diameter, it weighs ten tons and has twenty-four sets of glass prisms. You could see the light about twenty-two miles out and the glow from as far as seventy miles away."

Probably the largest and most powerful lens ever to serve in an American lighthouse, the huge bivalve is the pride of the Navesink Museum collection. Unfortunately, this unique and nearly priceless relic was severely damaged in 1991 in a mindless act of vandalism. A brick was thrown at the lens and shattered several of its delicate prisms. Repairs will cost $120,000, but eventually the lens will be on display again in the museum, where it can be enjoyed by one and all.

Navesink is no longer an official government light station. The beacon in the north tower was discontinued in 1894 when lighthouse officials decided to stop displaying lights in pairs. The south light served until 1953, when it, too, was extinguished. Today, a small sixth-order light shines in the south tower, but only as a way of honoring the station's long service tradition. Although it is of little use to mariners, the light is thoroughly appreciated by the museum's visitors— about 90,000 of them each year.

"It's a wonderful place to come on a beautiful afternoon and sit and watch the ocean," says Laverty.

A Right Smart O' Crab

I n rivers and estuaries mariners must grapple with a far different set of challenges than those facing them along the outer coasts. The narrow, serpentine channels of an inland waterway such as the Chesapeake Bay require a more subtle approach to navigation. Giant lenses such as the one at Navesink or tall towers such as the one at Fire Island are all but useless here.

With more than four thousand miles of shoreline, the Chesapeake is America's largest inland estuary. The importance of the bay's maritime commerce and its marvelously productive fisheries led to the construction of dozens of lighthouses. A century ago this was by far the nation's best-lit waterway. Because of erosion, ice, and improved technology, less than a third of the lighthouses built on the Chesapeake remain in use today. However, major ports at Baltimore, Norfolk, and elsewhere on the Chesapeake continue to attract their share of shipping, and the bay still supports its distinctive waterman's culture.

The term "commercial fisherman" is seldom heard on the gray wooden docks that push out into the Chesapeake from Maryland's tradition-bound Eastern Shore or the tributaries of the Potomac. "We don't call them fishermen," says Pat Vojtech. "We call them watermen. I think that's because we don't just fish here. We catch crabs, oysters, clams, and all different types of seafood."

Vojtech is a journalist and the author of *Lighting the Bay*, which tells the story of the Chesapeake's unique assortment of lighthouses. An inveterate sailor, she has seen nearly every inch of the bay and gotten to know its crusty watermen.

"Many go out in bad weather and they get caught," she says. "They judge themselves by how many bad storms they've weathered."

The Chesapeake watermen, a few of whom still work the bay in sailing vessels, are famous for their navigational skills. Those with the sharpest instincts are said to have "a nose for the water." It is not unheard of for them to find their way by the angle of the ripples on the surface and even by the taste of the water. By reading the signs just right and working from dawn until dusk, watermen may bring home baskets brimming with the bay's most prized delicacies: what they themselves might describe as "a right smart o' crab."

But even the most experienced waterman may occasionally rely on the help of a well-placed beacon. "Many of the lighthouses were built to guide watermen into the various rivers," says Vojtech.

Anyone who has ever sailed here knows that the Chesapeake is a bewildering maze of points and inlets. Its low-lying shores offer few distinguishing features, and when a ghostly afternoon haze rises from the water, as it does almost daily during the summer, the coast can be completely obscured in a blanket of gray. To find their way, navigators need all the help they can get. Beginning about two hundred years ago, that help appeared in the form of lighthouses.

The first Chesapeake lighthouses were conical stone structures such as those at Havre de Grace or Turkey Point. Most were not very tall because there was no need for their lights to reach far out to sea. Typically, the squat towers and keeper's residences were separate structures. Later, to save money, the government started building towers and dwellings in a single unit, usually a modest wooden house with a small lantern perched on its roof. But the most important innovation in lighthouse construction on the Chesapeake was made not to cut costs but because of the bay's unique geology.

Essentially, the Chesapeake is a flooded river valley. As ocean levels rose at the end of the last ice age, the plain of the Susquehanna River was inundated. Eroding soils from Pennsylvania, Maryland, and Virginia have covered the flat bottom of the bay in a thick layer of mud. In many places the mud and sands have mounted up to form shoals. "We do have quite a few treacherous shoals on the Chesapeake," says Vojtech. "You get into a bad squall and you can lose ships on those shoals very, very easily."

The Chesapeake's Graceful Water Bugs

Marking the Chesapeake's vicious shoals demanded fresh thinking and revolutionary construction techniques. Traditional shore-based towers would not do the job. The message of a mainland beacon could be misconstrued and carry a pilot into a shoal rather than away from it, and all too often an on-shore light could not be seen at all from mid-channel. The only answer was to build lighthouses directly over the shoals, but until about the middle of the nineteenth century, the technology for doing this was unavailable. Ordinary wooden piles could not be driven deep enough into the muddy bottom to hold up a tower.

Then, about 1850, engineers developed hardened iron piles with blades at the end that could be screwed deep into the mud. Six or more of these hefty screw piles would be twisted securely into the bottom to anchor and support a platform for a small keeper's cottage and tower. Usually the cottages were round or hexagonal and had a small lantern peeking through the center of their gabled roofs. Standing above the tides on their skinny iron legs, screw-pile lighthouses looked a bit like huge water bugs. In effect, they were tiny artificial islands, and their modest cottages were stocked with everything the resident crews needed to live and keep the lights burning for weeks at a time.

Although the screw piles solved the mud problem, they offered little protection from the massive ice floes that came rumbling down the Chesapeake in winter. Often, the floes ripped a vulnerable cottage right off its piles and sent the crew scrambling to abandon the station before it was crushed by the ice or sank in the freezing waters of the bay. Occasionally, lighthouse tenders or naval vessels would find the shattered cottage floating far down the Chesapeake, many miles from its naked piles. When possible, the lens and other valuable pieces of equipment were salvaged.

Time and technology also took a toll on the Chesapeake's open-water lighthouses. Many were replaced by buoys or abandoned when the Coast Guard determined their lights were no longer needed. Of more than forty screw-pile light stations that once marked the

The **Thomas Point Lighthouse** has stood on the
shoals of the Chesapeake Bay since 1875.

bay from end to end, only one remains at its original location: the striking Thomas Point
Lighthouse just south of Annapolis.

"There is no mistaking the Thomas Point Light," says Pete Lescher, curator of the
Chesapeake Bay Maritime Museum on the Maryland Eastern Shore. "It has a bright red,
hexagonal roof with a gable on each face." The station is remarkable in more than appearance. Built in 1875, it has survived everything the Chesapeake could throw at it. A sizable
mound of heavy riprap on the north and south sides of the structure have served successfully as an icebreak and blocked the destructive floes that have carried away so many of its
cousins.

The stone could not stop progress, of course, but the little lighthouse has been lucky.
Not automated until the 1980s, Thomas Point was the last light station on the Chesapeake
with a resident Coast Guard crew. Although its keepers are gone now, the lighthouse still
does its job, warning vessels of all types with its flashing red light to keep well away from
Thomas Point Shoal. "It still marks the main channel used by those modern container ships
going up to Baltimore," says Lescher.

The Thomas Point Station is not accessible to the public, but there are a number of
places around the bay where people can see and enjoy screw-pile lighthouses. One of these
is the St. Michaels, Maryland, museum, where Lescher serves as curator. There the hexagonal Hooper Strait Lighthouse stands on shortened iron legs waiting to delight visitors.

Pete Lescher

The Hooper Strait Lighthouse once guarded a key Chesapeake channel where it replaced an earlier screw-pile structure in 1879. "The first one got knocked off its foundations by the ice and sank rather quickly," explains Lescher. The lighthouse seen at St. Michaels today was more fortunate than its predecessor. "It actually had a long useful life," says Lescher. "It served until 1966 when it was slated for replacement by a pole light."

The old cottage was barely saved from destruction. The lighthouse had already been sold to a demolition contractor by the time the museum stepped in and purchased it. In order to move the forty-foot-wide building to St. Michaels, it had to be cut in half like a giant apple and loaded onto a barge. Now handsomely restored and furnished, it offers a glimpse at life in a turn-of-the-century light station. Living quarters and work rooms look as if the keeper left them only minutes ago and went ashore in a launch to pick up the mail.

Other screw-pile lighthouses can be found at the Calvert Marine Museum in Solomons, Maryland, where the 1883 Drum Point Light is on display, and in Baltimore, where visitors to the popular Inner Harbor can see the 1855 Seven Foot Knoll Light. Like the Hooper Strait Lighthouse, these historic structures no longer guide mariners. Instead, they serve as reminders of human inventiveness and past wars between man and nature.

For those who want to see real working lighthouses, the Chesapeake has a treat in store. There are still plenty of active navigational lights here. Several of the Chesapeake's original shore-based lights remain in operation. Beacons still shine from towers at Cove Point in Maryland, Old Point Comfort in Virginia, and elsewhere on the bay.

Less accessible but no less historic are the Chesapeake's caisson lighthouses. Built on massive iron and concrete platforms that might weigh several hundred tons, they were not so vulnerable to ice and weather as their more delicate screw-pile counterparts. The heavy

The **Hooper Strait Lighthouse,** one of only a handful of surviving cottage-style, screw-pile light towers.

caissons were towed out into the bay by barge and then lowered down through eighty feet or more of water and mud to the underlying rock. Designed for strength and durability, a dozen of the bay's caisson-style lighthouses have survived, and most are still fully operational. Their names are legendary: Wolf Trap, Point No Point, Sand Point, Thimble Shoal, Bloody Point Bar.

While no longer indispensable for navigation, these are no lifeless monuments. Sailors still need and appreciate their guiding beacons, for the bay remains a heavily traveled maritime highway—and a very dangerous place for ships.

A Comforting Blanket of Lights

For more than two hundred years, ships have been guided into the Chesapeake Bay by a light shining from Virginia's Cape Henry. The first navigational facility funded by the U.S. Congress, the Old Cape Henry Lighthouse was built by order of President George Washington. Completed in 1791, the ninety-foot stone tower cost the government $15,000 and proved in the end to have been quite a bargain. It served for almost a century before large cracks appeared in the lower walls, raising fears that the old tower would soon collapse.

A new and much taller tower was hurriedly built and ready by late in 1881. A 156-foot cylinder made of bolted cast-iron plates and

Cape Henry

lined with brick, it cost almost ten times as much as the earlier lighthouse. It was fitted with a first-order Fresnel lens that remains in use, flashing out the letter "*u*" in Morse code.

Interestingly, both structures still stand today. As it turned out, the Old Cape Henry tower far outlived the engineers who predicted its imminent demise. In fact, it remained in such good condition that it was restored and relit in 1972.

Almost in the shadow of these two grand navigational monuments is a much shorter, four-story building overlooking the beach, the ocean, and the Chesapeake shipping lanes. Although its appearance is modest by comparison to the soaring light towers, it is crammed with high-tech navigational equipment. Inside it looks much like an air-traffic control tower, and it serves essentially the same purpose. However, the vehicles guided by this

Black and white vertical stripes distinguish the 1881 **Cape Henry Lighthouse** from the station's original stone tower built in 1791.

These venerable structures keep watch over the entrance to the Chesapeake Bay.

tower are not airplanes but rather block-long ships. It is the dispatching tower owned and operated by the Maryland and Virginia pilots associations. Any large vessel of foreign registry must take on board a registered association pilot before entering the bay.

"We board the ship and assist the master," says Rick Amory, president of the Virginia Pilots Association. "When he boards a ship, the pilot carries with him local knowledge of the shoals, obstructions, currents, and hydraulic effects of the local channels."

Each pilot must serve a five-year apprenticeship, which in part accounts for the association's very select membership. At present, there are only thirty-six registered Virginia pilots. The Maryland Pilots Association maintains a separate registry of about the same size.

The pilots are well paid, and it is easy to understand why. Their work is challenging—and dangerous. The ships they guide must be boarded in open water several miles

Rick Amory

out from the cape where conditions are not always ideal.

"In good weather boarding is a piece of cake," Armory says. "But unfortunately, we don't always have blue bird weather. We have tremendous winds at Cape Henry and tremendous seas. But pilots have a way of putting the danger out of their minds. If they didn't, I don't think they could do this job."

Whatever the weather, getting onto the hulking freighters can be tricky. Most can be boarded only by means of a Jacob's ladder coiling thirty feet or more down the side of the ship. But the highly experienced pilots clamber deftly up the ladders. Once on the ship, they hurry to the bridge where their real work begins, that of guiding their assigned vessels through the winding and often dangerous Chesapeake channels to safe berths somewhere on the bay.

Maryland Pilots Association boat and tower

"We have all kinds of navigation equipment," says Amory. "We have satellites, Lorans, depth sounders, compasses—all these wonderful things. But when your eye sees that lighthouse at night, that red sector or that white sector, you know where you are."

"Cape Henry Lighthouse was here when I started my apprenticeship, and I have learned to depend on it as I think every mariner that comes in and out of here depends on it. Lighthouses have been around a long time. They are literally a beacon in the night. They are a comfort, a security blanket."

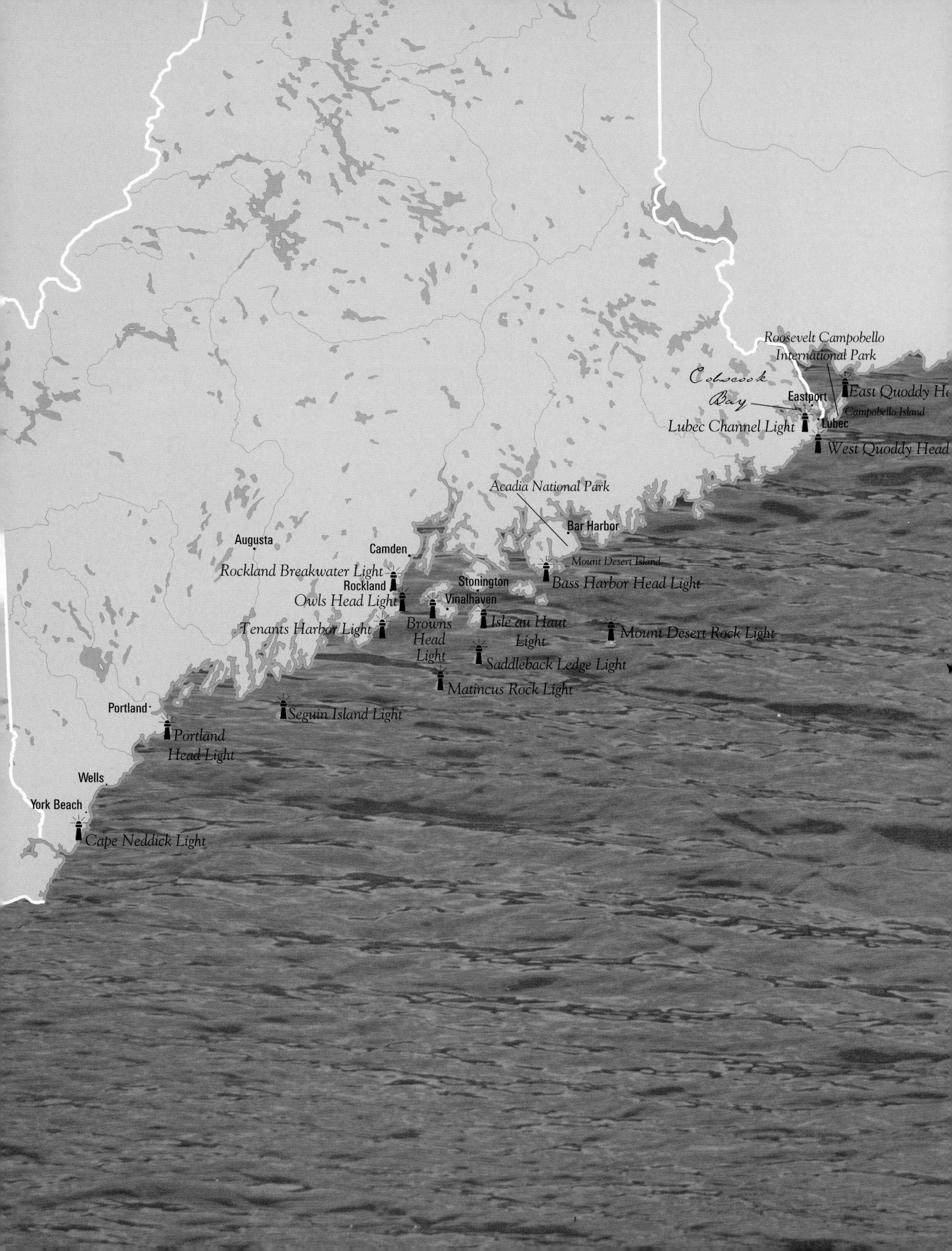

Roosevelt Campobello
International Park

*Cobscook
Bay*

Eastport

Campobello Island

East Quoddy He[ad]

Lubec Channel Light

Lubec

West Quoddy Head

Acadia National Park

Bar Harbor

Mount Desert Island

Augusta

Camden

Bass Harbor Head Light

Rockland Breakwater Light

Rockland

Stonington

Owls Head Light

Vinalhaven

Tenants Harbor Light

*Browns
Head
Light*

*Isle au Haut
Light*

Mount Desert Rock Light

Saddleback Ledge Light

Matincus Rock Light

Portland

Seguin Island Light

*Portland
Head Light*

Wells

York Beach

Cape Neddick Light

Saint John

Bay of
Fundy

Halifax

MAINE
Lights Downeast

A Memory of Ice

David Candee

Travelers are often surprised to discover that Maine is more east than north. Traditionally, New England sailors speak of the state as being "downeast" or even "way downeast." Maine trends toward the Atlantic, and this in part accounts for its extraordinary character. Land and sea come together here in a dramatic way, and for this reason, the hardy folk who seek a living along these rocky shores never take for granted the water, the solid earth—or one another. For this reason also, Maine is a place of many lighthouses.

Piloting his patrol boat through an inlet way downeast, David Candee points to a white metal cylinder poised on a massive black caisson. The Lubec Channel Lighthouse rises only a few dozen feet above mid-channel, and it is easy to see why such structures are often referred to as "sparkplugs." Indeed, this one looks as if it could be used in a fanciful advertisement for an automobile parts company. Established in 1890, the Lubec Channel Light is one of America's lesser-known navigational beacons. The lantern perched on its pudgy tower displays a green signal visible from not much more than six miles away, but despite its modest power, mariners rely on it to guide them through the narrow passage.

Out beyond the confined channel is a much older and more famous light station. Its eighty-foot tower made conspicuous by red and white bands, the West Quoddy Head Lighthouse stands guard atop a wall of ruddy cliffs cloaked in evergreens. A few hundred yards out from this bold headland, a blade of rock thrusts upward through the waves. From a distance, it looks like the sail of a small boat, but as more than a few sailors have unhap-

Lubec Channel Light

pily discovered, it is made of much harder stuff than canvas.

Whenever duty calls Candee out past Sail Rock, he gives it a wide, respectful berth. He is a boson's mate first class in the U.S. Coast Guard. Candee hopes to make chief petty officer soon, and almost certainly he will. He's dedicated to his work.

"A lot of times you're out in less than favorable conditions," says Candee. "So when you've finished the job, you pull the people out of the water, or you have the boat in tow, these lighthouses are like anchors. You know where you are and where you're going."

Knowing where you are and where you are going can be a tricky thing in Maine, particularly on the water. This state's incredible 3,478 miles of shoreline—about the same as California—is crammed inlet upon inlet into just 228 miles of coast. Mariners here are confronted with a maze of points, passages, reaches,

A harbor on the Maine coast

thoroughfares, bays, and coves, and nearly every channel is an obstacle course strewn with rocks, shoals, and small islands.

Glaciers created this labyrinth. During the last glacial era, a period of a hundred thousand years or more, ice piled up a mile thick over this part of the North American continent. Slowly grinding its way toward the ocean, the heavy ice bulldozed the underlying rocks, excavating deep trenches leading down to the sea. When the glaciers melted about ten thousand years ago, they left behind numerous long, slender peninsulas and narrow, fjordlike fingers of salt water reaching up to fifty miles into the heart of what now is Maine. Today, marking the end of nearly every peninsula or, conversely, the entrance to each lengthy inlet, is a lighthouse.

Clinging to craggy outcroppings at the edge of the sea or anchored to the bottom by metal caissons, these sentinels look natural rather than manmade, as if they grew up right where they stand. They didn't, of course. They were built, mostly during the nineteenth century, by highly skilled coastal masons and craftsmen. Their builders were the ancestors, perhaps, of contractors who nowadays line the shores with summer homes for out-of-staters—known in Maine as the "people from away."

Most of Maine's sixty or so major lighthouses are more than a hundred years old and some almost two hundred. But the maritime culture they serve is older still. Fishermen from Scotland, Ireland, and Wales first settled along these coasts during the century after the Pilgrims landed at Plymouth Rock in 1620. Like the tourists who now flock to Maine during July and August, they appreciated high-quality seafood, and here they found fish and lobster in wondrous abundance. Their descendants have continued to harvest the ocean's bounty for the better part of three centuries.

Over the years Maine's navigational lights have guided countless fishermen and other mariners to safety. They still do that—the job for which they were so carefully built—but today they also serve as a focus of interest for curious tourists, history buffs, and even PBS film crews.

Candee has seen nearly all of Maine's lighthouses from the water and more than a few up close. He lists them one after another as if ticking off the names of old friends on his fingers. "Heading up the coast, you go past Cape Elizabeth, then Monhegan, then Matinicus Rock, then Mount Desert Rock," he says. "And then home. Home is where you've got to get back to, and I guess the lighthouse is kind of a good thing to see."

Located on the easternmost point in the United States, the **West Quoddy Head Lighthouse** is painted with red and white bands to set it apart from other light towers along this rocky coast. Patches of Arctic tundra grow only a few yards from the station on this very chilly headland.

Candee's homing beacon shines from the West Quoddy Head Lighthouse—the red-and-white-striped one—which oddly enough, considering its name, is located at the easternmost extremity of the United States. Everything in the U.S. is west from here. Only a few miles to the west are the small fishing ports of Lubec and Eastport, where Candee is stationed. The flashing West Quoddy Head Light points the way to these villages and beyond to the broad, deep-blue Passamaquoddy Bay and the St. Johns River. It also warns vessels away from Sail Rock and helps orient coasting vessels headed toward Canada and the Bay of Fundy.

Established in 1808 by order of President Thomas Jefferson, the West Quoddy Head Light has guided fishing boats and freighters for more than 190 years. The tower itself is not quite that old, however. It dates to a major renovation shortly before the Civil War. No one is sure exactly when the tower received its distinctive stripes, but their purpose is clear. They set this lighthouse apart from neighboring navigational towers to the southwest along the Maine coast or to the northeast in Canada.

One of West Quoddy's nearest neighbors is a Canadian lighthouse located at the far end of Campobello Island just across the border from Lubec. It is known as East Quoddy Head Lighthouse, which explains West Quoddy's rather ironic name. Consisting of a cluster of modest buildings and a white, flat-walled tower emblazoned with an enormous red cross, the Canadian station clings to a small, barren island just off Campobello's northeastern tip.

Travelers who visit West Quoddy Head State Park and its lighthouse often cross the International Bridge at Lubec and drive out to see the Canadian station as well. But most tourists who go to Campobello have in mind another, better know destination: the Roosevelt Cottage. Franklin and Eleanor Roosevelt owned a thirty-four-room summer home on Campobello Island. It was there, in 1922, that the future president came down with the polio that left him permanently crippled. The cottage is now the centerpiece of the Roosevelt Campobello International Park, a memorial to F.D.R. and a symbol of cooperation between the United States and Canada.

Incidentally, it was President Roosevelt who, in 1939, placed all U.S. lighthouses in the hands of the Coast Guard, making them even more the concern of people such as David Candee. Before 1939 the nation's system of navigational lights had been for almost a century and a half the exclusive province of the U.S. Lighthouse Service. Accountable only to the Treasury Department, the Service had operated as a bureaucratic island within the increasingly oceanic U.S. government. But in 1939 the Lighthouse Service ceased to exist, and the far less insular Coast Guard took over America's guiding beacons.

Whether located offshore or on the mainland, lighthouses are themselves much like islands, and few are more cut off from things than West Quoddy Head. Secreted behind a thick forest of firs, the old brick tower and adjacent dwelling stand in complete isolation. Located ten miles from the village of Lubec, they are about a two-hour drive from the nearest city, Bangor, which has a population of only about 33,000.

No keepers live at West Quoddy Head anymore, and with its automated beacon and fog signal, the lighthouse does its job of guiding mariners without assistance from human hands. It stands guard alone over one of America's loneliest places. Visitors here can easily imagine they are on the far northern coast of Labrador or Alaska. Indeed, near the tower are a few patches of real Arctic tundra left behind by the glaciers after they retreated northward.

Lubec and the nearby town of Eastport are also island-like. With their weather-beaten clapboard homes and struggling businesses, these bucolic maritime communities recall an era far removed from our own beltwayed, cabled, Internetted, cell-phoned, and hot-wired world. They are among the few remaining outposts of the old New England seafaring culture. Here a ruggedly independent and centuries-old way of life is making its last stand.

"They are holding their own," Candee says of the fishing villages. "Holding their own."

Never Look Down

Connie Small knows what it means to hold on tight. Three quarters of a century ago she stood in a tossing boat staring doubtfully at a metal ladder leading from the water some thirty feet up to the service platform of Lubec Channel Lighthouse. Her husband, Elson, was an assistant keeper there, and he had brought her out to his duty station for a visit. Now she wished she was back on the mainland.

"I can't do it," she pleaded.

"Yes, you can," he assured her. "You take hold of the rung, and I'll be right behind you. Just don't look down."

Small climbed and did not look down, that is, until she reached the top. Now in her nineties, she recalls that first trip to the lighthouse. "I was so excited," she says. "Overjoyed that I had done something I didn't think I could ever accomplish. Then I made a mistake and looked down over the rail, and oh, all that elation went right into my toes. How was I ever going to get back?"

In time, Small got used to the routine challenges of lighthouse life, for over the years she would live in a number of light keeper's residences, all of them in Maine. Often working side-by-side with her husband, she would help maintain light stations at Avery Rock, Seguin Island, and St. Croix as well as Lubec Channel. Small's memories remain sharp, and she regularly shares her experiences as the wife of a lighthouse keeper with school and community groups. An author and lecturer, she has appeared more than five hundred times before rapt audiences of children and adults, throwing open for them a window on a now distant era and a way of life most find difficult to imagine.

"It was a hard life, a rough life," says Small. "The sea was rough. But the isolation was the worst part. For

Connie Small

three months at a time, I might not see anybody but my husband. I missed hearing people's voices. That was the hard part. But I found ways to get by."

One of the ways she found to cope with the loneliness was to draw closer to nature. She began to study the rocks, the trees, the weather, the sea life in the tidal pools near the station—everything around her. "My husband joined me in that," she says. "He was as interested as could be. And so we shared that and we forgot all the bad things that distracted us from being happy."

Just as her husband became a partner in her study of the natural world, she pitched in with him when necessary to keep the lights burning. "The light was like a baby," she says. "You tended it like a baby because people's lives depended on it."

Sometimes the Smalls' own lives were threatened. On one occasion Connie nearly had her arm torn off by a winch. On another, Elson got trapped when a freak wave flipped over the station

Connie Small climbing the Lubec Channel Lighthouse ladder in the 1920s

launch, pinning his legs. They both pushed with all of their strength, but the boat was much too heavy for them. Their only hope was that the flooding tide would help them lift the vessel off his ankles before Elson drowned. It did.

Theirs was not an existence that most would have chosen, but Connie Small knows why she chose it. She had intended to go to school and study art, but then one day her husband told her he was going to work for the Lighthouse Service. Since other members of her family had been keepers, she had more than an inkling of what that would entail. For Small it was easy then, just as it is now, to look beyond the generalized romance attached to lighthouses to the hard realities of life at the remote stations. For her, romance had an altogether more personal meaning.

"I looked at him," says Small. "And he looked at me in that way of his. And I said yes."

Islands in Time

Many of Maine's earliest settlers chose to live on islands. With the sea to act as a moat, they were protected from attack by Indians or interference by landlocked government officials. While living as close as possible to their source of livelihood, the sea, they could take full advantage of commerce with their fast ships and nimble schooners. But with the coming of the railroads during the nineteenth century, the locus of trade and population shifted to the mainland. Slowly the offshore villages emptied and the islands were abandoned. Today, only a few year-round island communities remain. Once there were more than three hundred of them. Now there are just fourteen.

Among the larger and more populous islands is Vinalhaven, located about fifteen miles east of Rockland. Three times each day from April through October and twice daily during the winter, a state-operated car ferry pushes into a wood and steel dock in Vinalhaven's Carvers Harbor. During warm weather months, the ferry is crammed with tourists whose aim is to escape the summer traffic and commercial hubbub along U.S. Highway 1 and, of course, to see a real Maine fishing village. They are not disappointed.

The harbor bobs with lobster boats, dories, and pleasure craft of every description. On shore, visitors will find an assortment of small fishing-related businesses, an old-fashioned lobster pound, and several unpretentious restaurants specializing, naturally enough, in the freshest imaginable Maine seafood. There is a better-than-even chance that any lobster you crack open here was still in the ocean earlier in the day. A small hotel and a couple of charming bed-and-breakfast inns provide housing for those who wish to stay overnight or who miss the last ferry back to Rockland—it leaves each afternoon promptly at 4:30.

More than a few who step or drive off the ferry during the summer own one of the seasonal homes or cottages scattered along the shores of Vinalhaven and several nearby islands. During July and August, summers-only residents, many of them refugees from Boston, New York, Philadelphia, Washington, D.C., and other centers of urban craziness, can double or triple the populations of places such as Vinalhaven. However, only a few could afford or would choose to live here year-round. Most have scurried back to the city long before the weather turns raw, which it can do as early as the first week of October. In the late fall Vinalhaven gets down to its bedrock foundation of approximately thirteen hundred hardy souls, and by almost any reckoning, they are a breed apart.

"Extremely independent and strong-minded individuals," says Susan Lessard, who feels she has earned the right to an opinion. She has been the town manager of Vinalhaven for the last five years. "The majority of our year-round residents fish for a living, but there are also caretakers, carpen-

Lobster fishing off the coast of Maine

ters, artists, and sculptors," says Lessard. It is an extraordinary mix, and she has found that working here requires a special touch. "You can't push self-employed people," she says. "They're used to making their own decisions. You can lead them, but you can't push them."

Lessard has plenty of her own decisions to make, most of them made more difficult by the practical inconveniences of living on an island. "How do you fix your roads if you have no material? How much salt and sand do you need for the winter? What do you do when your boats aren't running and the mail can't fly?"

Lessard's job is challenging, but along with it comes a privilege bestowed on very few people these days: she gets to live in a lighthouse. The Browns Head Light Station about seven miles north of the harbor is the official residence of the Vinalhaven town manager.

The station's thirty-nine-foot granite rubblestone tower was built in 1832. The one-and-a-half-story wood-frame residence dates to 1857. Like most lighthouse dwellings, this one is quite modest, but Lessard feels comfortable here. "Coming home to the lighthouse is coming home," she says. "It's a refuge from a job that requires an awful lot of public contact."

Even at home there is still plenty of work to do, since one of her duties is to maintain the lighthouse property. Occasionally, she also serves as an unofficial tour guide, answering questions for visitors who come to see the old light station. However, Lessard is not the official keeper here. The Coast Guard still looks after the fog signal and the light with its automated fifth-order Fresnel lens. But she is on hand to raise the alarm when there is a problem with the equipment.

Browns Head Light

On one recent foggy night, Lessard arrived home and found the lantern atop the lighthouse tower cold and dark. The foghorn was silent. She immediately telephoned the Coast Guard and was told that no help would arrive before morning. So there was nothing to do but wait. Wait and worry. Any one of Vinalhaven's lobster boats might be out there on the water. Any one of those "extremely independent and strong-minded individuals" she met everyday over morning coffee at the town offices or in the aisle at the IGA grocery market might be looking in vain for the light or listening for the fog signal and hearing nothing. There was no telling who might be out there.

"It was a very sleepless night."

Generations of earlier keepers who served here and at hundreds of other American lighthouses were no strangers to long nights without sleep. Lessard understands the sacrifices they made. And why. She also feels she shares something of their experiences.

"Living at a lighthouse is an education, and you start to develop a sense of the history," she says. "There have been keepers at Browns Head since 1857, and although the light is automated, I'm the current resident of this lighthouse. I'm part of its history, too."

Night of the Ducks

Mariners navigating the broad channel between the large islands of Vinalhaven and Isle au Haut will see a rusty tower rise apparitionlike from the rolling waters of the Penobscot Bay. This is the Saddleback Ledge Lighthouse, built in 1839 on barely half an acre of utterly barren rock.

One night in 1927 the Saddleback station's all-male crew was startled by a tremendous boom. The noise was so explosive that the keepers at first thought they were under attack by a foreign warship or submarine. Running to the lantern room to inspect the damage, they learned the truth. Their lighthouse had not been hit by an enemy shell, but rather by a wayward duck, and a very large one at that. The hapless creature, killed when it crashed through the lantern room glass, later weighed in at more than ten pounds.

The night had more surprises in store, for the air raid was far from over. Soon, entire flocks of ducks and geese were pummeling the lantern, breaking windows, knocking the keepers off their feet, and smashing into the station's delicate Fresnel lens. For a short while, the light was put out of action, but some fast work by the crew got it back in service quickly.

By morning a great heap of birds lay at the base of the tower. Some were only dazed, and these were placed in the station boathouse until they could recuperate and fly away. Others were found to be beyond help, and a few of those ended up on the dinner table.

The Saddleback Ledge Lighthouse clings to a scrap of barren rock in the eastern reaches of Maine's Penobscot Bay. The light is now automated, but for more than a century it was maintained by keepers who lived and worked in this isolated place. Wind and water have erased all traces of the station residence.

A Place Apart

Guests at the lighthouse on Isle au Haut, a mountainous island just to the east of Vinalhaven, may expect an exceptionally sound night of sleep unbroken by flocks of crazed ducks—or any other disturbance. That's right. This is a lighthouse that accepts guests and—if you can get them—reservations. This unique country inn is just the thing for anyone who has ever dreamed of living, even for a brief time, in a real Maine lighthouse. Known as the Keeper's House and operated by a pair of maximally relaxed innkeepers named Jeffrey and Judith Burke, it is the perfect place to really, really get away from it all and catch up on sleep. Where else could you drift off with a warm and comforting navigational beacon shining in through your bedroom window?

Of course, you have to be rather intent on getting there. Isle au Haut—the name is French for "high island"—can only be reached by way of a mail

Isle au Haut

Stonington Harbor

boat/passenger ferry from Stonington, which is itself quite a long way off the beaten path. Some believe Stonington to be the quintessential Maine fishing village, and they have an argument. But to those returning here after a week's stay on Isle au Haut, the quiet streets of bucolic Stonington may seem like midtown Manhattan.

The Burkes themselves once lived in New York City. They also spent some time in California and, when they were in the Peace Corps, Venezuela. For several years they operated a bed and breakfast in Pemaquid Point, Maine, not far from the lighthouse there. Then, in 1985, they continued their retreat from mainstream and Main Street America by moving to Isle au Haut.

"It was clear to me and Judi at the time that we'd stumbled quite by chance on a rather remarkable place," says Jeffrey Burke, "and an incredible opportunity." Seizing the moment, the Burkes took over the deteriorating Isle au Haut keeper's residence, restored it, and opened it as an inn. They have operated it successfully ever since. Although remote by almost any standard, the Keeper's House is invariably full during warm-weather months. And once they've stayed here, guests keep coming back. "The type of experience people

Poised at the edge of the tides, the granite base and white cylinder of the **Isle au Haut Lighthouse** mark the approach to one of Maine's pristine coastal islands. The station's historic residence now serves as a unique country inn where guests can enjoy good food and a taste of lighthouse living.

have here usually takes them by surprise," says Jeffery Burke. "We don't have telephones or electricity and no entertainment per se. That's the amenity we have—nothing."

Guests would say that what the Keeper's House offers is very far from nothing. Foremost among its many attractions is the setting. Isle au Haut is a wonderland of mountains, pines, and matchless ocean vistas. Much of the island is taken up by an almost untouched section of Acadia National Park. A hiker's paradise, this part of Acadia is blessedly separated by two dozen miles of seawater from the rest of the park on tourist-trampled Mount Desert Island.

Of course, the lighthouse itself provides much of the charm. Built in 1907 on a mass of volcanic rock known as Point Robinson, it was intended to guide fishermen in and out of the island harbor, a job it has done well ever since. The tower's sixteen-foot brick upper section rests on a twenty-foot-high base of granite blocks rising from the edge of the water. An elevated wooden walkway connects the tower to the two-and-a-half-story Victorian-style dwelling. The main residence contains four guest rooms, each simply, though comfortably, furnished with antiques. Two additional guest rooms are located in the station's restored oil house and barn.

As they bed down for the night, guests can enjoy the red-and-white glow of the beacon shining from the tower. The soft glow of the light seems to exert a mysterious influence on some of them. According to Jeffrey Burke, people often make life-changing decisions while staying at the inn.

"People have time to think here," says Jeffrey Burke. "To rejuvenate. We've had people decide to move, to leave the city, or to embark on some new adventure. We've had people propose to their sweethearts."

The good food at the Keeper's House may put guests in a romantic mood. The meals, prepared and served three times a day by Judith Burke, are delicious but not fancy—everything must be brought in by ferry from the mainland. "We try to keep it very simple," she says. "Kind of homey. We pack people's lunches, and they walk out the door saying 'Thanks, mom,' and things like that."

For Judith Burke, moving to the light station at Isle au Haut was something of a homecoming. She grew up in lighthouses. Her father was a lighthouse keeper on Nantucket Island, then later at Truro on Cape Cod. "You could see the light from my bedroom window," she says, thinking back on Truro. "So it's in my blood, I think."

Judith and Jeffrey Burke

Life on the Rocks

Some of Maine's light stations are even more remote than the one on Isle au Haut. In addition to Saddleback Ledge, already mentioned, there are several lighthouses still functioning on stony outcroppings such as Mount Desert Rock and Matinicus Rock. Located on barren islets under siege by the Atlantic, these towers are so far from the mainland that only experienced mariners and the most intrepid of tourists will ever see them. And yet, up until only a few decades ago, lighthouse keepers and their families lived on them year-round.

Since commuting from shore was impractical, the keepers kept their wives and children with them, and every member of the family faced the same hardships, dangers, and punishing weather. Usually, the family also shared in the heavy work of keeping the lights burning, often displaying the same heroic resolve as the keepers themselves.

Such was the case with Abbie Burgess, who grew up on Matinicus Rock some twenty-five miles from the mainland. One stormy night in 1856, young Abbie drew a chair to the kitchen table of the battered keeper's dwelling and dipped her pen into ink. A lonely seventeen-year-old, separated by half a day's sail from the nearest country store, barn dance, or church social, she had decided to write a letter to a pen pal on shore.

> *You have often expressed a desire to view the sea out in the ocean when it is angry. Had you been here on 19 January [1856], I surmise you would have been satisfied.*
>
> *Father was away.* [Keeper Sam Burgess had gone to Rockland to purchase supplies and, trapped there by a sudden nor'easter, was forced to leave his bedridden wife and daughters to weather the storm alone.] *Early in the day, as the tide rose, the sea made a complete breach over the rock, washing every movable thing away, and of the old dwelling not one stone was left upon another. The new dwelling was flooded, and the windows had to be secured to prevent the violence of the spray from breaking them in. As the tide came, the sea rose higher and higher, till the only endurable places were the light towers. If they stood, we were saved, otherwise our fate was only too certain. But for some reason, I know not why, I had no misgivings, and went on with my work as usual. For four weeks, owing to the rough weather, no landing could be effected on the rock. During this time, we were without the assistance of any male member of our family. Though at times greatly exhausted with my labors, not once did the lights fail. I was able to perform all my accustomed duties as well as my father's.*

Abbie Burgess

Few light stations are more isolated than the one on Maine's **Matinicus Rock,** a barren island about 25 miles from the mainland. The remote station was home to keepers and their families for more than a century. The stone towers date to 1857, but only the one in the foreground remains in use.

LEGENDARY LIGHTHOUSES

Established in 1795, the **Seguin Island Lighthouse** is one of America's oldest navigational stations. The enormous first-order Fresnel lens, in use here since 1857, remains in the lantern. The residence now houses a museum.

You know the hens are our only companions. Becoming convinced, as the gale increased, that unless they were brought into the house they would be lost, I said to mother, "I must try to save them." She advised me not to attempt it. The thought, however, of parting with them without an effort was not to be endured, so seizing a basket, I ran out a few yards after the rollers had passed and the sea fell off a little, with the water knee deep, to the coop, and rescued all but one. It was the work of a moment, and I was back in the house with the door fastened, but I was none too quick, for at that instant my little sister, standing at the window, exclaimed, 'Oh, look! Look there! The worst sea is coming.' That wave destroyed the old dwelling and swept the rock. I cannot think you would enjoy remaining here any great length of time for the sea is never still and, when agitated, its roar shuts out every other sound, even drowning our voices.

A few months after the month-long Atlantic storm described in her letter, Abbie Burgess married a young Lighthouse Service employee. Years later, she and her husband became keepers of the Matinicus Rock Lighthouse.

Eighty years and three generations after Abbie Burgess wrote her letter, young Tom Skolfield made his first trip to Seguin Island, located well to the west and south of Matinicus Rock and closer to shore. Skolfield was only eighteen months old when he was brought to the island where his father had recently been made a keeper. His arrival could not be described as auspicious. The thirty-three-foot Coast Guard launch he was riding in rolled over in the surf, drenching the boy and his five-year-old sister. Luckily neither of the Skolfield children was injured.

Despite its rough beginning, Skolfield's childhood on Seguin was a happy one. "It was like being Tom Sawyer," he says. "I had the roam of sixty-eight acres surrounded by water and half a mile of shore."

Usually, there were no children on Seguin other than Skolfield and his sister, but they found an ideal companion in the island itself. "It was a big island, and it took quite a while to walk around it. There were pools of water at low tide, and there were sea urchins and what I call Chinamen's caps—little suction cups that moved around on the rocks. And there was always something drifting in. Back in those days we had those big, round glass globes—floats from trawlers."

The children found plenty of things to do. "We improvised," he says. "With all the fishing lines we had, we could tie them together and put a kite almost out of sight."

Skolfield made a submarine with a handmade propeller on the front and a broken piece of shingle for a rudder. "I used to run that in the cistern down in the engine room when my dad was on watch."

Tom Skolfield

There was no electricity on the island and no refrigerator for keeping ice cream and the like, but Skolfield's father made an imitation ice cream treat for his family using an empty coffee canister. "He'd put some vanilla pudding in it and take it out and bury it in a snow bank. About every fifteen minutes, he would go out and stir until it was kind of icy. It wasn't really ice cream, but when you were out there [on Seguin] it was."

The Skolfield family left Seguin Island for the last time when Tom's father was assigned to a mainland station shortly after World War II. More than half a century would pass before Tom Skolfield saw the island and its lighthouse again. Recently, he returned just to take a look around, visit the museum that now occupies the keeper's dwelling where he used to live, and stir some reflections on his past.

"Everything was a little smaller than I remembered it," he says. Even so, he still found the station's enormous first-order Fresnel lens quite impressive. Among the more powerful lighthouse optics on the East Coast, the huge lens, made of many separate polished prisms, is big enough to fit "six to eight people inside it." His fondest memories, however, were of smaller things and personal experiences that might seem insignificant to others, for instance, sitting with his father in the fog signal building "while the engines were going and the horn was blowing . . . all night."

Thinking back on his lighthouse childhood, Skolfield will shake his head and say, "I had a pretty good life out there. Yep. A pretty good life."

LEGENDARY LIGHTHOUSES

The **Portland Head Lighthouse** has marked the entrance to the bustling harbor of Portland, Maine, since 1790. President George Washington and the Marquis de Lafayette were among the early visitors to this light station. Nowadays many tourists follow in their footsteps.

Christmas Lights in July

Even for those of us who never lived in one, a visit to a lighthouse can feel like going back home. The Victorian or early-twentieth-century dwellings seem a lot like our grandparents' or great grandparents' houses. Perhaps the homey, old-fashioned impression we hold of these historic structures is responsible at least in part for their increasing appeal. It seems that more and more people nowadays are fascinated by lighthouses.

Several of Maine's best-known lighthouses have become major tourist destinations. Among these is the Portland Head Lighthouse, located on an exceptionally scenic point of rock near the entrance to Portland Harbor. Not only is Portland Head the state's—and perhaps the nation's—most frequently visited lighthouse, it is also Maine's oldest light station. Completed in 1790, it was dedicated early the following year by the Marquis de Lafayette, the Revolutionary War general. Since then, the fieldstone tower has stood up to more than two centuries of pounding by raging Atlantic storms.

Today, the eighty-foot cylindrical tower and nineteenth-century keepers residence—now a fine museum—attract droves of camera-toting visitors, especially during Maine's brief but intense summer tourist season. The highly educational museum has on display the station's original second-order classical lens, which in 1989 lost its job and place of honor atop the tower to a modern, automated beacon. So beautiful is the old white tower and red-roofed residence that their likeness is endlessly reproduced on posters, calendars, T-shirts, and even boxes of cereal. For many, Portland Head seems the very ideal of a Maine lighthouse.

The same might be said for the Cape Neddick Light Station, also known as the "Nubble." Cape Neddick is the last, or most southwesterly, of the glittering chain of coastal lights stretching from West Quoddy Head, not far from the Canadian border, to York, only a few miles from New Hampshire. Like Portland Head, it is also among Maine's best known—and loved—lighthouses.

Established in 1879, the Cape Neddick Light Station was a hit with tourists from the beginning. Its location on a small, lovely island just off the wealthy summer cottage community of York Beach made it an attractive spot for picnics. The fantastic shapes of the island's wave-sculpted rocks captivated visitors who thought they saw faces in one or another them—George Washington was a favorite. There also was an odd formation known as the Devil's Oven and, as if to warn the devil against cooking up anything too evil, a nearby stone Preacher's Pulpit. But the lighthouse itself has always been the star of the Nubble show.

The Cape Neddick Lighthouse is an unusual and particularly handsome structure. Its forty-foot brick tower is sheathed in metal plates to protect it from the weather. An enclosed walkway connects the tower to the Victorian-style, clapboard keeper's residence. There are

The highly scenic **Cape Neddick Lighthouse** stands on a small stony island just off York Beach on the southwestern coast of Maine. A covered walkway links the Victorian keeper's dwelling with the cast-iron tower.

some marvelous touches here. Gingerbread detailing covers the eaves of the dwelling, and the balusters of the gallery railing near the top of the tower sport miniature, cast-iron lighthouses. Visitors with a sharp eye for directions will note that the ells of the main building form a cross precisely aligned to the north and south, east and west.

Travelers who drop by York Beach for a look at this wonderful old light station may have to satisfy themselves with a long, longing gaze from shore. The adventurous may think of wading across to the island, but this is dangerous and should not be attempted. The station is off limits to the public except for occasional tours offered by the Friends of Nubble Light, the nonprofit organization that now cares for the property.

During the holiday season, the York Parks Department outlines the tower and dwelling with Christmas lights, much to the delight of local children. The station is similarly bedecked in July for the benefit of tourists. But for the Friends of Nubble and others who love and appreciate lighthouses just for what they are, the beacon's red glow is decoration enough.

Long-time Nubble "Friend" Bill Thompson believes Americans find lighthouses irresistibly attractive. As he sees it, lighthouses represent "something people really can't touch." He thinks that hard-to-define something is a simpler, more natural "way of life they'd like to share."

As a young man, Thompson recognized, in his own boyish way, the marketing potential in lighthouses. During the summer, he took advantage of the crowds of tourists who gathered to admire the Cape Neddick Light by selling them tiny ships-in-bottles he had handcrafted. "I sold them for twenty-five cents," he says.

Bill Thompson

Lights in Bottles

Entrepreneur Tim Harrison has found lighthouses far more marketable—and profitable—than ships-in-bottles. His Lighthouse Depot shop and catalog sales operation in Wells, just up U.S. Highway 1 from York, has become an almost legendary Maine business success story. "About 250,000 people a year come through our store," says Harrison.

The big wooden sign near the door reads GIFTS, COLLECTIBLES, CLOTHING, VIDEOS, AND JEWELRY. Once inside, however, shoppers will discover there is more here than advertised, in fact, a positively dizzying array of lighthouse related items. If it can be made and is related to navigational lights, then the Lighthouse Depot has it. There are lighthouse candles, lighthouse lamps, lighthouse pins and bracelets, lighthouse mugs, lighthouse models, even lighthouses-in-bottles.

"We have over ten thousand different lighthouse items," says Harrison. "Lighthouse ties, clothing, hats, and limited edition collectibles. Everything from lighthouse toilet paper to dog biscuits shaped like lighthouses. You name it, and we've got it."

This unique, prosperous retail and mail-order business evolved from Harrison's own fascination with lighthouses. Years ago, when Harrison and Kathy Finnegan moved to New England from the Midwest, lighthouses became for them an important personal symbol. "Kathy wanted to visit every lighthouse in Maine," says Harrison. "We felt we could do this in an afternoon or two, not realizing that there are over sixty-eight lights along the coast of Maine, and most of those are in remote places."

Harrison and Finnegan soon learned that one of the things that makes lighthouses so appealing—their splendid isolation—also makes them very hard to reach. Many, as we have already seen, are on islands far from the mainland. Others are located at the end of unimproved roads, difficult to negotiate even in a four-wheel-drive vehicle. Undeterred by the logistics, the two set off on their lighthouse safari, picking their way along coastal backroads and tracking down one light tower after another.

"In the process we found that a lot of people were doing what we were doing," says Harrison, "Visiting the lighthouses and building their vacations around them."

Most were encountering the same problem of actually locating the light towers. To assist their fellow lighthouse hunters, Harrison and Finnegan decided to write a book. First

Tim Harrison and his Lighthouse Depot

published in 1985, it was called *Lighthouses of Maine and New Hampshire*. Before long, lighthouses became not just an interest for Harrison and Finnegan but a business. During the years after their book appeared, they opened the Lighthouse Depot, started up a far-reaching catalog-and-mail-order operation, and launched *Lighthouse Digest*, a monthly magazine with an international subscription list of lighthouse lovers and aficionados.

Not surprisingly, *Lighthouses of Maine and New Hampshire* can still be found on the shelves of the Lighthouse Depot. (Incidentally, among the extensive offerings in the Depot book section are eight regional lighthouse guidebooks and one recently published national guide written by Ray Jones, the co-author of *Legendary Lighthouses*, and illustrated with lush color photos by noted travel photographer Bruce Roberts.) Browsers will also find historic and technical volumes on towers, lamps, and lenses. And, of course, there is plenty of lighthouse-related human drama—shipwrecks and rescues, hurricanes and tidal waves, mysteries, disappearances, ghost stories, and fantastic legends.

Legend of the Frozen Lovers

Lighthouses are like aging movie stars. Nearly every one is associated with dozens of fascinating stories, all supposedly true. In Maine, where rugged shores and bold weather inspire drama, mariners have used their fertile imaginations and native eloquence to spin countless yarns based on the events of their daily lives. Sometimes lighthouses play supporting roles in these tales, but often they are at the center of them.

Among Maine's most delightful maritime yarns is that of the Frozen Lovers. It is still told in bars frequented by sailors, over midnight coffee in coastal diners, or in the waiting lounges of ferry stations. The story unfolds in the year 1850 near Rockland, about midway along the coast from York Beach to West Quoddy Head.

As with many tales of shipwreck and rescue in New England, this one takes place during a winter nor'easter. Blizzards are, after all, the very stuff of good stories, and that is especially the case in Maine, where bad weather is legendary. The pilots of boats caught in winter storms here claim that the spray from waves striking the bow freezes in midair and rattles when it hits the deck. Indeed, it often seems that glaciers are about to reclaim this state. Ice and snow can lock up vast stretches of the interior mountains and the coast for days if not weeks at a time. Massive bodies of coastal water have been known to

Rockland Breakwater Light

freeze over completely. Once during the 1920s, for instance, the entire Penobscot Bay froze solid. It is said that an adventurous motorist was able to drive a Model T across the ice from Camden, just north of Rockland, to Castine on the far shore some twenty miles away. But that is another story.

No doubt, ice and cold were the last things on the mind of a certain first mate when he proposed to a lovely young woman and then, one evening shortly before Christmas, invited her to his cabin on a small schooner anchored in Rockland Harbor. Only the mate, his bride-to-be, and a deckhand were aboard that evening. The captain and the rest of his crew had gone ashore, perhaps in search of a little holiday cheer of their own in one of Rockland's portside saloons.

Late that night, a vicious gale blew in off the ocean and snapped the schooner's anchor cables. The mate and deckhand fought valiantly to save their vessel, but the violence of the storm proved too much for them. A powerful wind drove the schooner relentlessly across the harbor, finally tearing open its hull on the cruel ledges not far from the Owls Head Lighthouse. Held in a vice grip by the rocks, the hulk filled with water but did not sink.

Trapped along with the wrecked schooner were the three frightened people huddled on its deck. Unable to reach shore in the boiling surf or to take shelter in the flooded cabins below, they were exposed to the worst the storm could throw at them. Drenched repeatedly by spouts of freezing seawater tossed up by the huge waves pounding the broken hull, their clothes grew stiff, and their skin turned rough and crusty with ice. They would soon freeze to death unless something was done to shield them from the spray.

In a desperate attempt to save themselves, the three rolled up in blankets and took what refuge they could beside the stern rail. As they had hoped, the spray soon encased them in a cocoon of ice, which helped protect them from the cold. In time, however, the fickle ice became their enemy once again. As the night wore on and the storm continued to howl, their frozen shells grew so heavy that it began to crush the life out of them. Eventually, they were entombed in a glistening layer nearly a foot thick.

Bundled together, the mate and his girl eventually lost consciousness, and by morning the deckhand believed he was the only one left alive. Slashing at the ice with a small knife and using his bleeding hands as hammers, he eventually managed to break free. Peering through the blizzard, he could see that the tide had gone out, leaving a narrow bridge of exposed rock leading to shore. Dropping down from the deck, he stumbled over slippery boulders toward the faint glow of the Owls Head Light. Cold and exhaustion overwhelmed him, and he was forced to crawl the last few hundred feet to the door of the keeper's residence. There the keeper found him, and in the warm kitchen of the dwelling, listened as the deckhand told his incredible story.

Although he had little hope of finding anyone alive aboard the schooner, the keeper quickly organized a rescue party and headed for the wreck. What he and his companions saw when they reached the shattered vessel left them speechless. The hull was painted in a ghostly white glaze. On deck, near the stern, were a man and a woman locked in a lover's embrace and frozen in a solid block of ice. Chipping away for nearly an hour with picks, shovels, and knives, they finally managed to free the couple.

Although everyone believed they were dead, an attempt was made to revive the pair. Hurried to a home not far from the lighthouse, their apparently lifeless bodies were treated with cold-water baths and massage. In two hours, the young woman regained consciousness.

An hour after that, the mate also showed signs of life. It took the two of them several months to recover from their ordeal, but by June they were both strong enough to stand in front of a minister and take their vows.

Unfortunately, the sailor, whose grueling trek had summoned help and saved the lovers from certain death, never fully recovered from his adventure and did not go to sea again. Living out his life on the Rockland waterfront, he told anyone who would listen about the great blizzard of 1850 and the frozen lovers of Owls Head.

In a Glass House

Some say Rockland's best and most prolific storyteller nowadays is Ken Black. A former commander of the Rockland Coast Guard Station, Black now runs the Shore Village Museum on Limerock Street. Although he is handy with words, Black's most eloquent statements are made through the poetic media of glass and light. His museum is filled to capacity with lighthouse lenses large and small. The largest is a big second-order Fresnel that once served at Petit Manan Island about eighty miles east of Rockland, but there are many smaller ones as well. Some of the lenses rotate, casting their white, red, or green glow around the several rooms of the museum.

Ken Black

"Everything here that can work, does work," says Black. "That's why children just love our museum."

And Black loves to show people, young and old, through his collections of lenses, bells, fog signal equipment, and lighthouse paraphernalia of every type. The sheer delight of the place returns even the stodgiest adult to childhood. Pointing to this flashing lens or that fog sensor, Black explains it all in clear, everyday language.

"Generally speaking, every lighthouse was before electricity," he tells a crowd of visitors gathered in the museum's front room. They have just gotten off a bus. "In the early days of this century, even if they had electricity they didn't use it simply because they had to generate their own and the generation of electricity was unreliable. Lighthouses had to be reliable because people's lives depended on them."

One guest asks Black about the different types of lenses. "No two lights in a general area can be the same," he says. "To make them different they sometimes put bull's-eyes in the lenses and made them go around. Every time the bull's-eye passes between you and the light—flash. It doesn't really flash. It just looks like a flash. The light is lit all the time." Black waits for everyone to acknowledge understanding, which they all do by nodding their heads. "Now just a few more things to show you in this next room," he says, and off he goes.

The extraordinarily knowledgeable Coast Guard skipper-turned-museum-curator can go on like this all day. And with wave after wave of visitors washing through the museum every day during the summer, he gets plenty of chances to share his expertise. "People have just gone crazy about lighthouses," says Black. "Especially during the last few years. Everywhere you look you see lighthouses. We're seeing pictures of lighthouses on boxes of shredded wheat."

Black admits that the interest of some lighthouse lovers runs to extremes. They have become, for lack of a better term, "lighthouse nuts." Black's own interest, however, is more educational and scholarly in nature. Can he help it if he occasionally gets caught up in other people's excitement?

Some years ago Black and his wife were in a boat up near the Canadian border. As they neared West Quoddy Head, Black's favorite lighthouse, he took the forty-foot vessel into the shallow waters between Sail Rock and the mainland. He was just sure his wife would want a close-up view of the colorful tower. Unfortunately, the tides were not cooperative that day. The boat struck bottom, dislodging a radio antenna that came down with a whack and struck Mrs. Black a glancing blow in the head.

"She wasn't too pleased about that," says Black. "But then, that sort of thing doesn't happen very often.

Castles Beside the Sea

Winding through a maze of moored lobster boats and pleasure craft, Peter Ralston confidently guides a sleek, well-maintained cruiser across Rockland Harbor and out into the lower reaches of the Penobscot Bay. It is something he does often, and although not a professional mariner, Ralston is as familiar as any full-time seaman with the bay's rough waters and tricky currents.

As much as twenty-five miles wide at its mouth, the bay was once a river valley. When sea levels rose as the glaciers melted at the end of the ice age, the valley was flooded, leaving a broad plain of water broken here and there by many small islands and a few larger ones. The islands here in the Penobscot Bay and elsewhere along the Maine coast have been the focus of Ralston's life for more than fifteen years. In 1983 he helped found the

Peter Ralston

Island Institute, a nonprofit organization dedicated to the preservation of Maine's natural and cultural island heritage. He is the institute's executive vice president.

"The Island Institute was established to offer services to the island communities here in Maine," says Ralston, "services that recognize there is something special going on in these islands. People here are in touch with how their great grandparents lived and made their living from the sea."

The institute does what it can to help keep that way of life intact, to hold back what Ralston calls "the rising tide of homogenization" that has swamped the rest of America. It is no small undertaking, and Ralston's work takes him out on the water frequently. Today's destination is Green's Island, where he will check on one of the institute's long-term projects—a lighthouse.

As a matter of fact, this outing, like most boat trips in coastal Maine, could be considered a lighthouse sightseeing expedition. As the institute vessel exits the harbor, the Rockland Breakwater Lighthouse emerges from a dense fog bank. Except for the small circular lantern perched on its roof, the building looks like an ordinary brick home. One might think that it was, in fact, a Rockland residence that somehow slid into the water and floated out into the bay. The truth is, it was built in 1902 exactly where it stands on a massive stone base at the end of a mile-long breakwater. Keepers did live there once, but not anymore.

"As it has done virtually everywhere else, the Coast Guard automated the light and removed the crew," says Ralston. "It's kept in relatively good shape. However, the inside has been let go and it's pretty grim." Ralston hopes the town of Rockland will soon take possession of the breakwater lighthouse and thoroughly renovate it. He thinks it would make a fine small museum, a destination for the hundreds of hikers who walk out on the breakwater each day during the summer.

Opposite the breakwater, a natural arm of stone extends several miles into the bay, defining the south side of the Rockland Harbor. At its end, a rock formation takes the shape of an owl with tufted ears and hooked beak—or so it is said. During the summer, tourists flock to the rail of the Vinalhaven Ferry and strain their eyes to catch a glimpse of the big bird. Nearly everyone claims they can make it out quite clearly, but they each seem to be looking at a different part of the headland, seeing, it seems, what they want to see.

Ralston does not bother looking for the owl. What fires his imagination is the far more obvious structure rising from atop the rugged headland like the turret of a small medieval fortress—the 172-year-old Owls Head Lighthouse. Built 1826, during the presidency of John Quincy Adams, it is one of Maine's oldest—and shortest—light towers. Only about twenty feet tall, the little lighthouse barely peeks above the stunted trees that cling to this windswept promontory. But its light can be seen from sixteen miles at sea in clear weather, and its foghorn is one of the most powerful anywhere. The horn is so loud that it can damage hearing, and light station visitors are warned to clamp their hands over their ears in foggy weather.

"Over the years, tens of thousands of ships have found their way into this harbor in thick fog, storms, and the dead of the night, thanks to that light," says Ralston. "Thanks to that fog signal. Tens of thousands of ships."

Ralston says that his attitude toward the Owls Head Lighthouse and to navigational lights in general leans away from the romantic and toward the purely functional. "I'm not sen-

Wyeth and Ralston

Tenant's Harbor Light

timental about them," he says. "My interest in lights has always been far more practical. I'm on the water all the time, twelve months a year, and if I lose the electronics in my boat, the Loran and radar and so forth, I know there will still be a light or there will still be a horn."

On the other hand, Ralston understands that lighthouses are an important symbol. "People who live hundreds of miles from the ocean, who will never have to rely on a light or a fog signal as an aid to navigation still get what lighthouses are about," he says and then lists some of those things: "Vigilance. Caring. Being there. Helping other human beings."

Ralston contrasts America's historically important lighthouses with the castles that have stood on European hillsides since the Middle Ages. "Unlike the castles in Europe, which are wonderfully symbolic, historic edifices, lighthouses still serve their original purpose," says Ralston. "Lighthouses do still save lives." As if to emphasize Ralston's point, the Two Bush Light winks red from the southern horizon. To the east another light calls from Browns Head on Vinalhaven.

Ordinarily, the crossing to Green Island would take about an hour, but today Ralston has allowed time for a detour. He is stopping off to visit an old friend who lives on Southern Island near Tenants Harbor just down the coast from Owls Head. His friend is the artist Jamie Wyeth, who, by coincidence, happens to live in a lighthouse.

Wyeth and Ralston exchange warm greetings outside the nineteenth-century Cape-style keeper's residence where Wyeth has lived and painted for nearly a decade. The two have known each other since they were children growing up in Chadds Ford, Pennsylvania.

"Jamie and I are very close," says Ralston, who regards Wyeth's parents, artist Andrew Wyeth and his wife, Betsy, as his own "second parents." It was the Wyeths who introduced Ralston to Maine during the late 1970s. A photographer, Ralston immediately fell in love with the state, its people, and its folkways. "Andy and Betsy challenged me to 'go deep,' and I've been doing that along this coast for the past eighteen years."

In a sense, Ralston sees himself as following the Wyeths' example. "Their entire lives revolve around a ten-mile radius from their studios," he says, "tight little worlds in which they have done master work after master work."

In short, the Wyeths are *island* artists. "I've lived on islands all my life," says Jamie Wyeth. "It tends to give me more focus in my work."

For years Wyeth lived and worked on Monhegan Island, home to one of Maine's more vibrant and traditional fishing communities. Most houses there still have no electricity. Although Monhegan continues to provide subjects for Wyeth's paintings, he has lived on

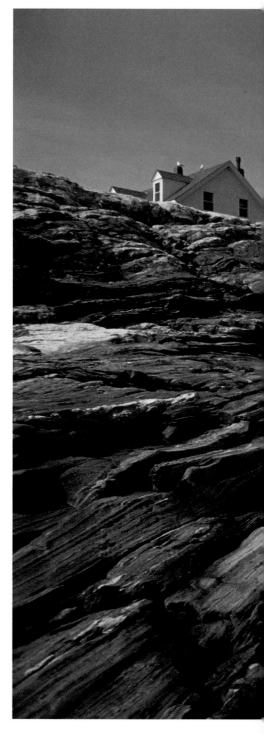

Southern Island since 1990. That year, Wyeth's parents vacated the Tenant's Harbor Lighthouse, which they had owned for many years, and moved to another, more remote island. Jamie Wyeth, looking for a place even quieter than Monhegan for his studio, moved in behind them.

"My mother did most of the restoration work here," says Wyeth. "And you know, for a while it did look like an Andrew Wyeth painting." Now the younger Wyeth has invested the old lighthouse with his own unique personality and vision. Even so, he still occasionally feels he is living inside an oil painting. "Living in a lighthouse is living in a cliché. There's no question about that. But I happen to have a lighthouse on this island. It's wonderful looking. I use it in my paintings. So I don't care if it is a cliché."

A man's home is, after all, his lighthouse.

Fire on Heron Neck

L ater, Ralston is back out on Penobscot Bay and soon approaches another island and yet another lighthouse. It's the Heron Neck Light Station on Green's Island not far from Vinalhaven. He goes ashore in a dinghy and follows the plank walkway leading to the top of a rose-colored granite cliff where the tower and dwelling stand at the edge of a grassy field. These structures sport a fresh coat of white paint and show signs of extensive recent repairs. Ralston takes obvious pride in the improvements, as well he should. This lighthouse belongs to the Island Institute.

Ralston explains how a nonprofit educational organization concerned primarily with schools, fisheries, and environmental legislation came to own a remote island light station. "Lighthouses have never been at the core of the institute's mission," he says. "We had never done any hands-on work with them until the Heron Neck Lighthouse burned in April 1989. There was an electrical fire here, a bad fire—windows burned out, floor burned through, a great gaping hole in the roof."

The damage was so severe that the Coast Guard decided the structure wasn't worth repairing. Dating to 1853, the station was no more historic than most lighthouses. With all the

Carved into fantastic shapes by glacial ice, the rocks in front of the **Pemaquid Point Lighthouse** look a bit like ocean waves, but they would tear apart any fog-blinded vessel that sailed onto them. The light here has warned ships away from these deadly formations for more than 170 years.

Heron Neck Light

radar and other pinpoint navigational electronics crammed aboard ships nowadays, its beacon was certainly not indispensable. But when the Coast Guard announced its plan to tear down what remained of the old building, residents of nearby Vinalhaven objected. So, too, did lobstermen who frequented the waters around Green's Island. Soon, preservationists on the mainland joined the public outcry. It seemed the Heron Neck Lighthouse had more friends than anyone, particularly Coast Guard officials, had thought. At first the protests were ignored, but then the Island Institute joined the fray. "I rustled up a television crew," says Ralston.

Prodded by the institute, a Portland, Maine, television station assembled a news story on the lighthouse and its plight. "They came out here and filmed it," says Ralston. "It was a wonderful spring day. There were daffodils coming up and little lambs bleating and carrying on. It was very compelling, and—it actually made *The Today Show*."

Soon, cards, faxes, and telegrams from Heron Neck supporters came pouring in, and the more or less well-meaning Coast Guard found that it had stumbled into a hornets nest. The plan to demolish the lighthouse was put on hold.

Of course, that was not the end of the story. Money had to be found to repair and maintain the lighthouse. Strapped for funds by early 1990s federal budget cuts, the U.S. Coast Guard could not afford to restore the building. Four years of negotiations ensued during which it often seemed the lighthouse would be destroyed after all, if not by Coast Guard wrecking crews, then by the elements. The hard Maine winters were taking a toll on the exposed building. Finally, a solution was found.

In 1994 Congress authorized transfer of

the property to the Island Institute, which in return was to raise the money to save the building. The Coast Guard would continue to look after the light. To help the institute with fund raising, Jamie Wyeth provided three hundred signed prints of his painting *Iris at Sea*—a depiction of his own Tenants Harbor Lighthouse. Noted fiber artist Shirley Bridges donated an extraordinary lighthouse quilt. In the end the Heron Neck Lighthouse was saved.

Learning from this success, the federal government and local interests, including the institute, have now applied the same process to nearly thirty endangered Maine lighthouses. As part of what is being called the Maine Lights Program, the Coast Guard will keep the lights burning, but it is transferring ownership of the buildings to towns, municipalities, and private groups better able to care for them. Similar programs are now being organized in other states, and literally hundreds of historic wonders may be saved in this way.

Curri...

Kitty Hawk

Outer Banks

Bodie Island Light

Cape Hatteras
National
Seashore

Buxton

Ocraco...

Myrtle Beach

Charleston   Morris Island Light

Charleston Light

Savannah   Tybee Island Light

Sapelo Island Light

Brunswick

Amelia Island Light

Jacksonville   St. John's River Light

St. Augustine Light

Daytona Beach

Ponce de Leon Inlet Light

Cape Canaveral Light

Tampa

St. Petersburg

West Palm
Beach

Miami   Cape Florida Light

Fowey Rocks Light

Key West Light

SOUTH ATLANTIC

Graveyard of the Atlantic

Lights in Time and Space

Mostly flat and featureless, America's southern Atlantic shores seem deceptively gentle. There are no rock-strewn inlets here as in the Northeast, no lofty cliffs dropping precipitously into the sea as in the West. One might think this a relatively safe place for mariners, but nothing could be farther from the truth. This coast is extraordinarily dangerous, especially for mariners navigating in the dark or caught in the grip of a storm. Over the centuries, its vicious shoals and shallows have swallowed up uncounted thousands of ships and lives, earning for it a sinister reputation.

But this most perilous and—in its own way—dramatic of American shorelines is known for something else as well. It was here that navigation changed forever. Because of events that took place on this coast not all that many years ago, darkness will never look the same again.

The importance of the South to both the history and the future of navigation came into clear focus one summer day about thirty years ago when a giant rose up over one of Florida's sparkling white Atlantic beaches. A metal cylinder more than three hundred feet tall and thirty feet in diameter at the base, it pointed skyward in near perfect perpendicular alignment. An elegant and potent invention, it represented the highest technology of its era. Among its other astounding capabilities, it could brighten the sea and the land for miles in every direction.

Its light was a by-product of liquid hydrogen and oxygen rushing together to combust explosively and generate thrust—enough to lift a tall building. The date was July 16, 1969, and the cylinder was a Saturn rocket. In an Apollo capsule atop the rocket were Neil Armstrong, Edwin Aldrin, and Michael Collins, three mariners setting off on a mission like none before in the history of mankind. They were on their way to the moon. On their 500,000-mile round trip, they would navigate much as mariners have done for thousands of years—by taking readings on stars.

The reddish glare of the historic Saturn/Apollo-10 launch lit up the walls and windows of another metal cylinder only a few miles from the Kennedy Space Center. Although not

Cape Canaveral Light

nearly as tall or imposing as the Saturn rocket, it was roughly the same shape and it, too, reached for the sky. When it was built more than a century ago, it, too, was considered a technological marvel. With its smooth, white cast-

Old Glory flutters outside the keeper's dwelling at **St. Simons Lighthouse** in Georgia. Although a lighthouse stood here as early as 1810, the existing 100-foot brick tower dates to 1872. The station's original third-order Fresnel lens remains in place.

iron tower and powerful nautical beacon, the Cape Canaveral Lighthouse has been guiding mariners since just after the Civil War. When completed in 1868, the 168-foot tower was fitted with a first-order Fresnel lens, which represented the highest navigational technology of *its* era. The classical Fresnel has now been replaced by an automated beacon of more recent design, but its light can still be seen up to twenty miles away, nearly as far as the flaming exhaust of space center rockets.

During the early years of the U.S. space program, famed rocket scientist Wernher von Braun often climbed the lighthouse steps to view launchings from the tower's lofty gallery. Ironically, some of the missiles von Braun sent into space carried satellites that would revolutionize the way mariners on Earth found their way from place to place. Today, guided by signals from these "lighthouses in the sky" and their own shipboard radar, navigators know where they are at all times, regardless of the weather. They now have electronic eyes that can penetrate even the thickest fog bank and make night the same as the day. All of this has rendered the beacons of lighthouses, such as the one at Cape Canaveral, less critical for safe navigation.

Even so, navigational lights remain important as visual reference points and as a way for captains, pilots, and navigators to double-check electronic readings. And of course, seamen are happy to have the lights there to show them the way when radar and other shipboard guidance systems go on the blink—as occasionally happens. Only a generation ago, however, lighthouses played a far more crucial role in the life of the mariner. At times, they were his last, best hope of reaching port safely.

Ghost Mountains

America's first lighthouses were built during colonial times, mostly in the Northeast. These early stone towers—on Little Brewster Island in Boston Harbor, at Sandy Point near the mouth of the Hudson River, at New London, Connecticut, and elsewhere—were intended primarily to attract commerce and guide ships into a particular port. Erected on solid rock foundations, they were rarely more than a hundred feet tall, and in the early days, their lights were produced by simple tallow candles or oil lamps with reflectors. Marking the nation's southern shores would require a more advanced approach.

The lighthouses established along the southern coast beginning at about the turn of the nineteenth century were something new and exciting. Tall and technically innovative, they were their own era's equivalent of a space program. And without them, the waters of the South would have been all but unnavigable.

There is no coast on Earth quite like that of the American South. The declining, outer edge of a low-lying coastal plain that may stretch two hundred miles or more inland, the sandy beaches and mudflats along the southern shoreline started out as mountains. More than a hundred million years ago, a chain of mighty peaks, perhaps as lofty and massive as the Himalayas, stood where the stooped and grandfatherly Appalachians lie today. Seas rolled right into the foothills, and sharks patrolled where peaches, cotton, rice, and sugar cane now grow. Over the eons, the South's primordial mountains eroded, filling in the shallows with their mass and pushing the ocean steadily eastward. This process created soils of extraordinary richness—to the benefit of generations of farmers—and estuaries teeming with shrimp and crab—a blessing to fishermen. But it also built up a labyrinth of sand bars and shoals to haunt the seamen who came calling at southern ports to load the holds of their ships with the region's rich produce.

The ghosts of the South's prehistoric mountains are the mud and sand banks that lurk just beneath the surface all along the southern coast. These phantom shoals appear and vanish without warning, but they will crush the hull of a ship just as quickly and surely as any rocky shoal in Maine, any volcanic headland in California. Without beacons to guide mariners and warn them of these dangers, the coasts of the Carolinas, Georgia, and Florida would have been all but unnavigable. But before the nineteenth century brought a flurry of lighthouse construction, these remained dark and foreboding landfalls. Countless sailors and hapless passengers paid with their lives for the absence of lights to guide their vessels.

There are few experiences so profound as total darkness. A swirling liquid, it lifts you up and spins you around. It cuts you off from the world you know and sets you adrift in an ocean of black ink where there is no north or south, east or west, up or down. On the sea, darkness can be especially terrifying. Even so, sailors have seldom been afraid to go abroad at night. In fact, the evening sky was once the best friend of mariners since there was a natural chart and compass up there to guide them. But on those nights when fog rolled in or clouds drew an opaque canopy overhead, they sailed with little sense of direction, and it was best to keep as far away from land as possible. To approach the southern coast of the United States on such a night meant death.

Graveyard of the Atlantic

Using her bare hands as shovels, Lloyd Childres uncovers what looks like the remains of a floating log. Time and salt water have considerably damaged the wood. Rotten and pulpy, it breaks away freely, filling the brown beach sand with splinters and chips.

"These beams sticking out of the sand right here look like a wreck," says Childres. "You can see a line of beams along here like part of the side of a vessel."

Retired from her job as a historical preservationist for the state of North Carolina, Childres now serves as executive director of the Outer Banks

Lloyd Childres

A first-order bull's-eye Fresnel lens glows in the lantern room atop the 163-foot **Currituck Beach Light** tower on the North Carolina Outer Banks.

Conservationists, a nonprofit organization that maintains the Currituck Beach Lighthouse near the northern end of the long line of barrier islands known as the Outer Banks. The beaches near the lighthouse are littered with the remains of ships that wrecked in the shoals and shallows just off shore.

"Let me just see what we have," says Childres, continuing her digging. "Yeah, there's no doubt that this is a wreck. You can see some of the holes there where the planks were attached to the ribs. It looks like these were probably cedar beams. Or maybe oak."

Reaching nearly seventy miles out into the Atlantic, the North Carolina Outer Banks form one of the world's most deadly navigational barriers. Over the centuries, thousands of vessels, large and small, have come to grief here. The ruined hulk Childres now examines is only one of many now buried in the Carolina sands.

"It seems to me this was not too large a vessel," she says. "It was probably a two-masted schooner of about two hundred tons and with a beam of about thirty-four feet. Not a huge shipwreck, but probably one typical of the period."

Childres believes the wreck dates to approximately 1870, about the time the Currituck Beach Lighthouse was built. There is no telling now what ship this was, what it carried, where it came from, or where it was headed. One thing is clear, however—the ship never reached its destination.

Childres imagines the final hours of this now nameless and long forgotten vessel. "They were probably cutting it a little too close, thinking the Gulf Stream was closer in than it was or maybe trying to take advantage of the winds. Then they hit a bar maybe five hundred or six hundred yards out."

Once trapped in the Outer Banks sands, a vessel was doomed. The surf would tear it apart in a matter of minutes. "Once they hit the bar, things would have started to go," says Childres. "Things on deck—big barrels of water, wine, or whale oil—would have started to slide. The masts would go, the sails would start to shred, and there would have been a lot of shouting."

Probably the crew tried to abandon the doomed ship. "Sailors would have gone into the water," says Childres. "People would have been grabbing for lifeboats, hatch covers, and anything they could hold onto."

A wrecked sailor's chances of survival were not high, especially in the pounding surf of the Outer Banks. "It would have been a very scary thing," explains Childres, "especially in the dark. In the dark you're at the mercy of all of the elements, and you can't find the shore."

No one knows how many sailors or passengers lost their lives in disasters like this one, but historians agree that the toll has been very high. Entire crews disappeared without a trace, leaving no one to tell the story of the ship and its tragic end. Often, all that remained was a crushed hull and a few planks and pieces of rigging scattered along the shore.

Usually, after a wreck, part of the cargo washed up onto the beach. "There were whole families on the Outer Banks who survived by salvaging the cargo from wrecked ships and selling it at auction," says Childres.

Once the salvageable cargo was removed, the wreck was left to rot and sink into the sands. Occasionally, the wind and tides wash them up again. "Wrecks are appearing and disappearing all the time along these beaches," says Childres.

These rotting timbers are all that remain of some hapless vessel that wrecked long ago on the Outer Banks—known to mariners as the Graveyard of the Atlantic.

In recent decades Currituck, Kitty Hawk, Nags Head, and other Outer Banks communities have seen rapid development. Tourists flock here during warm-weather months, and the hotels, restaurants, and shopping malls built to accommodate them now stretch for miles. There has been a boom in home construction as well. Every year hundreds, if not thousands, of new houses are built just behind the beach dunes. Eerily, many of these homes stand right on top of the decaying ribs of ships, the relics of more than four hundred years of maritime calamity.

"I'm sure that there's probably not a house up here that doesn't have a ship wreck in its basement," says Childres. "Yes, I think you could say that people here live in a graveyard—in the Graveyard of the Atlantic."

Bodie Island Light

Interestingly, Childres now keeps a house that was built to prevent shipping disasters. Strategically placed about halfway between the Cape Henry, Virginia, and Cape Hatteras Lights, the Currituck Beach Lighthouse illuminated one of the last remaining dark stretches along the southern coastline.

"They had the wonderful Hatteras Light, but there was a tremendous dark spot between it and the light at Cape Henry," says Childres. "With the number of wrecks increasing, they needed a light to fill that sixty- or seventy-mile stretch, so they built this lighthouse here at Currituck Beach and the one at Bodie Island."

Currituck Beach Light

The Currituck Beach tower was completed in 1875 and was the last major lighthouse built in North Carolina. To help the tower stand up to the Atlantic's raging storms, it was given walls almost six feet thick. So that mariners could easily distinguish it from other lighthouses along this coast, its red bricks were left unpainted. The station's original first-order bull's-eye Fresnel lens remains in place. The automated light flashes white every twenty seconds and can be seen from up to nineteen miles at sea.

The well-maintained Currituck Beach Lighthouse is one of the South's most splendid historic structures. Its lush surroundings and red bricks photograph beautifully. Visitors with strong legs are allowed to climb the more than two hundred steps—for a small fee—to the gallery where they can get an up-close look at the station's priceless first-order classical lens. There they can also enjoy an expansive view of the lovely Outer Banks beaches—and burial ground for ships.

Boyhood at Bodie Island

As the mighty Gulf Stream sweeps past the Outer Banks, it pushes in close to shore. Since they wanted to avoid fighting its powerful northeasterly current, the captains of southbound ships often steered perilously close to land. When they came too close, the results were predicable—and disastrous. Following the Civil War, the government built a series of unusually tall towers on the Banks to warn mariners and help them keep their ships at a safe distance. These sentinels included the 158-foot tower at Currituck Beach, a new 193-foot tower at Cape Hatteras, and the 166-foot Bodie Island tower.

Two earlier lighthouses had stood at Bodie Island. Noted contractor Francis Gibbons completed the first tower here in 1848. He later built more than a dozen lighthouses in the West. Ordered by tightfisted government officials to drive no piles, Gibbons erected the tower on a muddy foundation, and it began to lean queasily out of plumb almost as soon as it was completed. Repeated efforts to right the structure failed, and it eventually collapsed into the sea. Its replacement, built in 1859, had stood for only a couple of years when it was blown up by Confederate troops during the opening months of the Civil War.

The soaring tower seen here today was built on a solid granite foundation set atop iron pilings and a grillwork of pine timbers. The technique proved successful, and the magnificent, black-and-white-banded tower still stands straight today. Although automated in 1931, its original first-order Fresnel lens remains in place.

John Gaskill remembers the light before it was automated. Now in his eighties, Gaskill lived at the Bodie Island Station with his family during the 1930s. His father, Vernon Gaskill, was the keeper.

Gaskill and his brother, Vernon Jr., were fascinated by their father's work. "We watched every

Bodie Island Lighthouse by moonlight

duty he performed," says Gaskill. "We'd come up with him sometimes in the evening to light the light."

During the days before automation, the process of lighting the station's five kerosene lamps was involved and touchy. "It was a little complicated," states Gaskill. "You had to use a torch to vaporize the kerosene. If it went into the lamps as a liquid, it would probably break the mantles. They were very, very fragile."

In 1931, the kerosene lamps were removed and an electrical lighting system installed. "They put in two little generators, like home lighting plants, and a big battery," Gaskill says. Ironically, the lighthouse residence was not wired for electricity at that time. "We continued to use kerosene lights in the house." Although the Bodie Island station was rustic and remote, Gaskill and his brother found plenty to do here. "It was kind of a good life," he says. "Our chores kept us busy, and in our free time we went fishing, boating, and beachcombing."

The Gaskill brothers also got into their share of boyish trouble. One of their favorite games was to race down the tower's spiral staircase, taking the steps four and five at a time. On one occasion Vernon Jr. fell hard and bit his tongue. "A little piece of his tongue was left hanging," says Gaskill. "Dad took the scissors he used to trim the torch and cut it off. It didn't affect my brother's speech any, but he had a little less tongue than he had before."

Among the more exciting times at Bodie Island was when the government lighthouse inspector made one of his "surprise" visits. "Usually we would know if an inspector was coming, because the first lighthouse he hit, they'd send word," says Gaskill. "Then everybody would get busy."

Today, more than half a century after Vernon Gaskill worked here—and occasionally scrambled to fix the place up for inspection—the Bodie Island Lighthouse still looks to be shipshape. Although the Coast Guard still maintains the light, the National Park Service keeps the grounds and dwelling open as an attraction of the Cape Hatteras National Seashore. The keeper's dwelling now houses a small museum and bookstore.

Grandfather Hatteras

Not far off North Carolina's famed Cape Hatteras, two mighty rivers slam into one another. The cold-water Labrador Current runs down the northeast coast of the United States, while the steamy waters of the larger and more powerful Gulf Stream flow in the opposite direction. The two collide just off the Outer Banks with a violence that has thrown up killer shoals and claimed thousands of ships over the centuries. Especially dangerous is Diamond Shoals, an enormous subsurface sand bank reaching about fifteen miles seaward from Cape Hatteras.

The barber-pole stripes of the 1870 **Cape Hatteras Lighthouse** spiral skyward over North Carolina's Outer Banks. Erosion threatens the 193-foot light tower, America's tallest. Each year high tides wash in closer to its vulnerable foundation.

To warn mariners away from the shoals and the threatening Banks themselves, one of the South's earliest lighthouses was built on the sands of Cape Hatteras. Completed in 1803, the ninety-five-foot stone tower was never very effective at keeping ships away from the shoals. A lighthouse inspector once described it as "the worst light in the world."

As part of a general upgrade of lighthouses on all American coasts, a new tower was built at Cape Hatteras in 1870. A soaring, 193-foot brick cylinder, it was painted with distinctive black-and-white, barber-pole stripes. The original tower was left standing, but in time, it was undercut by erosion and tumbled down onto the beach.

Some fear that the 1870 Hatteras Lighthouse, the tallest light tower in America, will suffer the same fate as its predecessor. Storm-driven waves have steadily cut away at the beach, bringing high tides to within a hundred feet or so of the tower. Unless something is done to protect the venerable building, its foundation may be undermined, causing this old coastal giant to collapse onto the beach.

For the time being, however, Outer Banks visitors can still see and enjoy what is perhaps the most famous and best-loved lighthouse in America. The tower stands just off Route 12, the main Outer Banks highway, and near the village of Buxton. One of the old keeper's dwellings houses a visitor center and museum.

As with many lighthouse adventures, the experience of getting to Cape Hatteras is as fascinating as actually being there. Highway 12 runs down through the Cape Hatteras National Seashore, a seventy-mile-long stretch of pristine beaches and dunes. The highway threads the narrow Outer Banks island chain, only three miles wide at its widest, carrying visitors far out to sea with the open Atlantic to the east and the mainland almost out of sight to the west. The fishing and birding here are perhaps the best to be found on the East Coast.

Buxton, Rodanthe, and some of the other villages on the Banks date to colonial times. It was here, on Roanoke Island, that the English planted their first colony in the Americas— it failed when the Roanoke settlement's tiny population vanished around 1590. Fort Raleigh Historic Site near Manteo commemorates the ill-fated colony and its disappearance. The Wright Monument near Kitty Hawk celebrates another, more recent and perhaps even more momentous historic event: the first powered human flight.

Light on Blackbeard's Island

To the south and west of Cape Hatteras is Ocracoke Island, home to one of North Carolina's oldest island communities. Founded in 1753, Ocracoke has a character and spirit all its own. Since it can only be reached by way of a lengthy ferry ride from the mainland or a somewhat shorter ride from remote Cape Hatteras, Ocracoke is indeed a "place apart." And at the center of Ocracoke—literally and figuratively— is its lighthouse.

"The lighthouse is part of the community," says Christina Kurth, a local potter. "It's the backdrop for everything."

In 1803, the same year the original Cape Hatteras tower was completed, a lighthouse was built on Shell Castle Island near Ocracoke. It stood not far from the inlet where the notorious pirate Blackbeard had been cornered and killed by colonial forces in the early 1800s. Destroyed by lightning, the original structure was replaced in 1823 by the existing sixty-five-foot conical brick tower. Automated in 1955, the Ocracoke Lighthouse remains in operation, displaying a fixed white light seen from fourteen miles away.

Ocracoke Light

But for residents of Ocracoke—only about seven hundred people live here year-round—the lighthouse is far more than a mere navigational marker. "It's in the middle of the village and has life on four sides of it," says Kurth. "It's surrounded by homes, cemeteries, and people's lives."

Life on remote Ocracoke is lived at a slower tempo than on the mainland. According to Kurth, that was always the case. "People would never leave the island," she says. "So they used to pack their overnight bags and walk over to relatives' houses to go visiting. They would stay overnight and make a real adventure out of it."

Until recently there were never many cars on Ocracoke and very few improved roads. Most people got around on foot using a network of trails and paths that linked one house

Christina Kurth

to another. Kurth's favorite path leads to the side of the island facing Pamlico Sound. "The trees grow over this path, and it really looks like you're coming to a paradise beach," she says. Instead of a paradise, the trail ends up near Teach's Hold. This is the place where the renegade Edward Teach—also known and feared as Blackbeard—was killed. A wealthy Englishman, Teach apparently got bored with his comfortable life as a British aristocrat and took to the sea as a pirate. It is said he had fourteen wives. For decades Teach ravaged the sea lanes connecting Europe with the New World. Then, in 1718, a pair of colonial warships trapped the pirate in his hold. Blackbeard's men fled into the marshes while he himself was shot and run through repeatedly with swords. "He was killed right here off Springer's Point," says Kurth. "They chopped off his head and threw it overboard."

Today, it is hard to imagine Blackbeard using this place as a hideout. Electric signs and street lamps call too much attention to the place, throwing up a glow that can be seen from far out at sea. In fact, their brightness now competes with that of the lighthouse beacon. "Before, when it really was dark here at night, the lighthouse had a very large presence," explains Kurth. "There were times when I'd stay up late at night and read by its light."

Even now people on Ocracoke sometimes find themselves reading or eating with the help of a candle or other emergency light source, perhaps even the lighthouse beacon. "We're way at the end of the line," says Kurth, "and we have a lot of power outages. A good Ocracoke resident always knows exactly where to find the matches, the candles, or the oil lamps."

Tourists staying on the island may feel inconvenienced by the occasional outages, but Ocracokers don't. "People think they're coming to the end of the world out here, and really they're coming to the center of it," says Kurth. "You know, I never had that feeling of being unsafe because of the dark. And I think that was partly the lighthouse."

High Water at Charleston

Charleston, South Carolina, has been visited often by calamity. Fire, hurricane, earthquake, and war have repeatedly pummeled this old Southern port city, but it has absorbed their blows with remarkable resilience and grace. Buildings may crumble, but they are always rebuilt or replaced, and life goes on.

It seems quite natural that a city so familiar with disaster should have built one of America's earliest lighthouses. A copper plate on the cornerstone of the city's original light tower—now in ruins—reads, THE FIRST STONE OF THIS BEACON WAS LAID ON THE 30TH OF MAY 1767 IN THE SEVENTH YEAR OF HIS MAJESTY'S REIGN, GEORGE III. This 1767 lighthouse was destroyed during the Civil War. Now the tower that replaced it is also threatened.

In 1876 a 161-foot brick tower was built on Morris Island, near the entrance to Charleston Harbor. Having survived a devastating earthquake in 1885, it served until 1962, when its responsibility for guiding mariners was passed along to the modern, concrete Charleston Lighthouse on Sullivans Island some distance to the east. Today, the abandoned Morris Island tower stands on the brink of ruin, its black-and-white bands faded and its foundation awash in the tides. A victim of rampaging erosion, Morris Island itself has all but disappeared.

But there are those who remember the Morris Island Station in its

Morris Island Light

active years. One is Gladys Meyer Davis, who lived on the island when her father was keeper there in the late 1920s and early 1930s. "I was born and raised at lighthouses," says Davis, whose father had worked at a series of Florida lighthouses before being assigned to Morris Island. "So was my whole family. I have one sister and a brother that were born at St. Augustine Lighthouse. I was born at Ponce de Leon Lighthouse, and my youngest sister was born at Jupiter Lighthouse."

Gladys Meyer Davis

By the time she was four or five years old, Davis's family had left Florida and moved to South Carolina. She has fond memories of Morris Island. "It was lush and tropical—a paradise really. It was a great place for a child."

Davis remembers many happy times on the island—visits from her grandparents who lived nearby on the mainland and rides over the dunes in her father's Model-T Ford. "He lashed two rowboats together, put the Model-T on them, and floated it across the river to the island," she says. "I'm sure people who saw it wondered how in this world that car got over to the island."

Of course, all was not play. There were many chores to handle. As did the children of many other lighthouse keepers, Davis and her siblings helped run the station. "Everything had to be white-glove clean, and that was our job, my sisters and I," says Davis. "My two brothers were responsible for going up in the evening and taking the curtains down so the light could shine out to sea. That was their job."

The older children had to be ferried across to the mainland each day to go to school. Almost certainly, they would have preferred to spend their days on the island with its dunes, beaches, and fishing. "It was a wonderful life," recalls Davis.

But just as childhood itself is brief, so too was Davis's idyllic life on Morris Island. Erosion had been steadily eating away at South Carolina's coastal sands, and the island itself was doomed. Most of it was swept away by a storm-driven tidal surge in 1935.

"It just devastated the whole area," says Davis. "I can remember looking out the upstairs window and seeing everything floating. The water seemed to be getting higher and higher." When the tide went out again, most of Morris Island was gone. "We lost our German Shepherd, Wolf," says Davis. "We lost the little kitten that Wolf had adopted and used to carry around. We lost my dad's pigs, turkeys, chickens, and what have you. And we lost the thing dearest to my dad: his Model-T."

Forced to the mainland, the Davis family moved to Charleston. In 1937 Davis's father was transferred back to Florida's Ponce de Leon Inlet Lighthouse, where he had once served as assistant keeper. During World War II, the Ponce de Leon keeper's quarters were taken over as a barracks by the Coast Guard, and the family moved into a house about two blocks from the station. Davis still lives in that same house today.

Georgia's Singing Lighthouse

On Tybee Island, about twenty miles east of Savannah, Georgia, is a lighthouse that sings. When a brisk wind blows, as it often does along the Georgia coast, the nearly two-century-old tower lets its voice be heard. Historic preservation specialist Cullen Chambers is familiar with the old tower's music and has even been known to "tune" the structure by opening and shutting certain windows.

"One of the things I noticed when I first got to Tybee is the unique sound it produced," says Chambers, who manages the Tybee Island Historic Site and is in charge of restoration projects at several other significant Southern lighthouses. "Initially I thought someone was at the top of the lighthouse playing a radio. But as I climbed, I realized that this was not an artificial sound. It was the wind blowing through the open windows, and it had a very musical quality."

Chambers wonders if similar natural sounds may be responsible for some of the ghost stories linked to lighthouses. "The ghost stories and mysteries associated with lighthouses

may be caused by wind blowing against or through the structure," he says.

The Tybee Island Lighthouse seems as likely a place as any in America to be haunted by a ghost. The history of this navigational station reaches all the way back to the founding of the colony of Georgia in 1733. Shortly after General James Oglethorpe brought settlers here from England, he ordered construction of a tall wooden tower to mark the entrance of the strategic Savannah River. Located on Tybee Island, the tower was destroyed several times by storms and fire, but it was always rebuilt. In 1791 the tower was fitted with a lamp, and it became a lighthouse. That same year, fire consumed the wooden light tower, scorching the keeper as he fled. "It was so hot I was not able to tarry for a moment," the keeper told his superiors.

Soon rebuilt with brick, the Tybee Island Lighthouse became one of several early light stations placed under control of the new federal government. Repaired

Shining from atop its 154-foot octagonal tower, Georgia's **Tybee Island Light** warms this peaceful early evening scene.

and restored several times, most notably after retreating Confederate troops burned it in 1861, the 154-foot octagonal tower still stands today. Its twelve-foot-thick walls have enabled it to resisted numerous hurricanes and an earthquake, but even so, time has taken its toll.

"Lighthouses were designed to be maintained on a regular basis by on-site keepers," says Chambers. "Since this lighthouse was basically abandoned in 1970, there has been no outside maintenance. In fact, Tybee Lighthouse hasn't been painted in over twenty years. Moisture has entered the building and caused decay."

Chambers points to the many wounds suffered by the two-century-old lighthouse. A sizable crack in the massive walls of the tower recalls a major nineteenth-century catastrophe: the great Charleston earthquake of 1885. "The earthquake struck South Carolina and moved down the eastern seaboard south of Charleston and damaged a lot of these old brick lighthouses. Masonry lighthouses were made to withstand just about everything—hurricanes, storms, and winters—but they were not really designed for earthquakes."

Cullen Chambers in Lamp Room

Lack of maintenance has been the structure's worst enemy, however. Chambers sees evidence of neglect everywhere. "Light keepers would never have allowed the walls to look like this," he says. "They always kept things whitewashed." Chambers thinks old-time Lighthouse Service inspectors would be aghast if they could see the condition of this and many other historic towers nowadays. "These buildings would certainly not pass muster," he says.

The Lighthouse Service was a spit-and-polish organization, at least when inspectors paid one of their unannounced visits to a light station. "People have this misconception of light keepers living a very relaxed life," says Chambers. "In fact, they worked under one of the most regulated bureaucracies in American government. There were actually white-glove tests where district inspectors would come in and literally inspect for dust, debris, and any sign of uncleanness or poor work habits. There were a couple of cases where light keepers were actually fired because the district inspector found their personal living quarters untidy and thought living that way would carry over into the keeper's work habits."

The Tybee Island Lighthouse would not pass a white-glove inspection nowadays, but fortunately, the historic structure is not being left to decay. The Tybee Island Historical Society and other organizations and government agencies are working to restore it. Says Chambers, "The idea is to restore the lighthouse to its former glory. I want to see this thing gleam again. I want to believe that, when we get it restored, it's going to pass inspection."

Light on Wild Island

With its expansive lakes of tall marsh grass, clean beaches, and gnarled coastal oaks, Georgia's Sapelo Island is a natural wonder. Certainly it is one of the wildest and most beautiful of America's coastal islands. The Georgia Department of Natural Resources maintains much of Sapelo as a wildlife and nature preserve and offers a variety of nature walks on the island. Until recently, these tours focused almost exclusively on the local flora and fauna, but now they often include visits to another of the island's treasures—its 175-year-old lighthouse.

Buddy Sullivan, manager of the Sapelo reserve, is an expert on both the island and its lighthouse. "Sapelo is a 16,000-acre barrier island," says Sullivan. "It's ten miles long from north to south and about the size of Bermuda."

Sapelo Island Light

Buddy Sullivan

Sapelo's isolation has shielded it from the development that has engulfed much of the coast elsewhere. "It is very isolated," says Sullivan. "The only access is by water. We have ferry service from the mainland twice a day, and that is really the only way to get over here. There are no roads to Sapelo, no bridges, and it has always been that way."

The remote island harbors a unique African-American community of former slaves. "The four-hundred-acre Hog Hammock is essentially the only privately owned land on Sapelo," says Sullivan. "There was a plantation here during the antebellum period, and many of the seventy-five or so residents of Hog Hammock are descended from the slaves who worked on it."

Built in 1820, Sapelo's lighthouse guided freighters to small Georgia ports such as Darien, where they loaded rice, sugarcane, and other products from plantations like the one here on the island. "The lighthouse had a sixty-five-foot tower and twelve-foot iron lantern," says Sullivan. "It cost the federal government $14,500."

No doubt, the ongoing effort to restore the lighthouse will cost much more. Badly damaged by a hurricane in 1898, it was deactivated, and a small steel light tower was built nearby. By the 1930s, shipping activities along this stretch of coast had decreased and the government abandoned the steel-tower light as well. "The lighthouse remains an important daymark," says Sullivan. "It has been here for over 175 years, and it is an important symbol."

Lighthouses on Canvas

Among those working toward restoration of the Sapelo Island Lighthouse is artist Bill Trotter. Since 1980 Trotter has been painting lighthouses all over America. "I painted ships, steamboats, nautical scenes, and so forth," says Trotter, "but lighthouses captivated me, and I wanted to do an in-depth study of them. The more I got into them, the more I realized this part of our history was going to be lost if we didn't do something about it."

Bill Trotter

For Trotter, doing something about it meant packing up his paints and brushes and heading out on the road. "One day I mentioned to my wife that I sure would like to go out and paint lighthouses," says Trotter, "and she said, 'Let's sell everything and go.' And that's what we did. People thought we were nuts."

Now Trotter has been traveling and visiting lighthouses for nearly twenty years. "I've visited a minimum of 350 lighthouses," he says. "When I see one I haven't seen before, I get turned on. It's just kind of like a kid with a new toy. I say 'Oh boy, here's one I haven't painted.'"

Trotter believes his paintings are helping to popularize lighthouses and raise interest in restoring them. "My role in preservation is keeping the history alive," he says. "And the way I do that is through painting. I'm an educator—in the art sense. I educate through my art. I see it as a way of helping to bring back part of the history."

Lighthouse Lew

In 1820, the same year the Sapelo Island Light began operation, a similar lighthouse was built on Little Cumberland Island in southeast Georgia. The latter served until 1838, when government officials had it dismantled and shipped to Amelia Island in northern Florida. There, near the mouth of the St. Marys River, it was reassembled. Renovated in classical Victorian style in 1885, the graceful sixty-four-foot brick tower still stands today, and its flashing white light remains in service guiding mariners through Nassau Sound.

Unlike many lighthouses, this one is in mint condition, thanks in part to the efforts of the local Coast Guard Auxiliary. Faced with tight budgets and increasing demands on its limited resources, especially in the area of lighthouse maintenance, the Coast Guard often relies on the assistance of its auxiliary flotillas. Lew Eason is a member of Auxiliary Flotilla 14 in Fernandina Beach, and he oversees volunteers who help maintain the historic Amelia Island Lighthouse.

"We keep watch on the lighthouse when the Coast Guard is absent," says Eason. "They come up once a month and do functional checks, but most of the time we keep an eye on it for them and make sure it's operating."

Amelia Island Light

Eason got involved with the lighthouse more or less by accident. "My wife and I bought a boat, and we didn't know anything about boats," he says, "so we joined the local Coast Guard Auxiliary because they offered a fantastic safety course in boating."

At about that time the Coast Guard approached Flotilla 14 and asked for volunteers to help with maintenance at the Amelia Island Lighthouse. Eason felt a special tie to the old tower, so he stepped forward. "The lighthouse is a part of Fernandina," he says. "It's part of our heritage here on this island, and so I felt quite privileged to do this."

Eason coordinates four teams that do work at the lighthouse or keep watch over it on a rotating schedule. The teams are composed of Auxiliary members, most of them retirees. Members have given Eason a nickname: Lighthouse Lew.

Lew Eason

The members of Eason's teams are not paid for the work they do here, and none of them seems to care—least of all Eason himself. For him, the job is its own reward. "In the mornings, when you come through the gate of the light station, the first thing you hear is the chatter of birds," he says. "Then there is the knocking of a red-headed woodpecker on the telephone pole. It's real therapy. I mean, you forget the week. You forget your job. You forget any problems around the house. It is so serene that you just want to stand here and take all of it you can get for as long as you can get it."

St. Augustine's Skydiving Kitten

Soon after the United States acquired Florida from the Spanish in 1821, government officials took possession of an old, four-story tower in St. Augustine. It may have been only a coastal watchtower, but some believe it once displayed a navigational light. If so, it would have been one of the earliest lighthouses in America. During the early 1820s, the U.S. government took possession of that same tower and remodeled it, placing a lamp and reflector on its top story. This beacon guided mariners right up until the Civil War, when it was darkened by Confederate forces. Tidal erosion eventually destroyed the historic tower.

By 1874 the government had replaced the original structure with the splendid 165-foot brick tower that still stands here on Anastasia Island. It was equipped with a first-order Fresnel lens—the same one that still focuses the station's beacon. For more than 120 years now, this light and the tower itself—distinguished by black-and-white, barber-pole stripes—have made the coast near St. Augustine safer for mariners.

Today, the old keeper's residence houses an excellent maritime museum that draws a steady stream of visitors. But this handsome station has long been attractive to tourists. When they lived here during the 1930s and early 1940s, Cardell (Cracker) Daniels Jr. and his sister Wilma (now Wilma Daniels Thompson) earned dimes and quarters by serving as guides. Recently, the two returned to the St. Augustine Lighthouse to share some of their memories.

With its spiral-striped tower and classically styled keeper's residence, the **St. Augustine Lighthouse** is a popular tourist attraction.

"Daddy [St. Augustine keeper Cardell Daniels Sr.] would let us take tourists up to the lighthouse and make us a bit of money," recalls Thompson. "We'd go up there and get tips. You couldn't charge back then, but we did it for tips. We'd get nickels, dimes, and quarters sometimes—enough money to go to the show and buy popcorn."

Keeper Daniels was never reluctant to let his children handle the tours, because his duties kept him busy. According to Daniels, his father stayed thin climbing the tower's 219 steps. "He kept his weight down by running up and down the lighthouse," says Cracker Daniels. "You never see a fat lighthouse keeper."

When not in school or leading tours, the Daniels children found plenty to do on Anastasia Island. "During the summertime, we'd just stay on the beach, go fishing, sailing, and mess around like that," says Daniels. These activities included some mischief. Once Daniels fitted out the family kitten with a toy parachute and dropped the hapless feline from the tower. "He didn't hit the ground too hard," says Daniels, "but as soon as he did, he took off through the scrub oaks. It was about three weeks before he showed up again."

Symphony of Color

Artist Bill Trotter says, "There is nothing more aesthetically beautiful than a lighthouse beehive lens. Like a diamond, it takes light and transforms it into a rainbow, a symphony of color that surrounds you whether it's at the top of a lighthouse or on exhibit in a museum."

Travelers who would like to see classical lenses up close should add the Ponce de Leon Inlet Lighthouse and its Sea Museum to their Florida itineraries. The museum houses one of the finest collections of lighthouse lenses in the country and is a good place to learn about the intricacies and history of Fresnel technology.

The Ponce de Leon Inlet Lighthouse has quite a history itself. This place was known as Mosquito Inlet when its first lighthouse was built in 1835. Before its lamps were ever lit, the tower collapsed in a storm. No further attempts were made to mark the inlet for more than fifty years, but during the 1880s, the government decided to establish a major coastal light here. Built with red brick shipped south from Baltimore, the 168-foot tower was completed in 1887. The new station was equipped with a fine first-order Fresnel lens, which shone brightly until it was replaced by a smaller, third-order lens in 1933. About that same time, Mosquito Inlet was given a new and decidedly more appealing name: Ponce de Leon Inlet.

In 1970 the Coast Guard discontinued the light, passing its duties along to a smaller light mounted on a steel tower at nearby Smyrna Dunes. Construction of a tall building soon blocked the new beacon, however, and the Coast Guard decided to recommission the old lighthouse.

Today, Ponce de Leon's flashing beacon is produced by a plastic lens. With its tower, residences, and outbuildings beautifully restored, the Ponce de Leon Light Station now comprises one of the best lighthouse museums in America. Not the least of its attractions is its

Lens Exhibit Building. Among its dazzling displays are the third-order lens used at Ponce de Leon Inlet from 1933 to 1970 and the enormous first-order clamshell Fresnel that once served at Cape Canaveral.

Jim Dunlap

"We got the Cape Canaveral lens in 1993," says Sea Museum curator Jim Dunlap. "The glass was beginning to fall out. Cape Canaveral had a special problem. Whenever they had a launch [at the nearby Kennedy Space Center], it was like a small earthquake."

To spare the huge lens any further damage, the Coast Guard removed it from the Cape Canaveral tower, replacing it with a modern optic. Now the huge Fresnel is on permanent display at the Sea Museum. Recently, it has been joined by another massive first-order Fresnel, one with a special significance for the Ponce de Leon Inlet Light Station. It is the very same lens that served here from 1887 until 1933.

"We thought that it had been dumped at sea, to tell you the truth," says Dunlap, speaking of the magnificent first-order Fresnel. "In 1933, when they electrified our light,

The massive brick base of the 168-foot **Ponce de Leon Inlet** tower on Florida's east coast. The nearby Sea Museum contains an extraordinary collection of Fresnel lenses.

they took this lens out and put it into storage at the lamp shop in Charleston, South Carolina. Sixteen years later it was loaned out to a museum in New England, where it sat in a warehouse for fifty-one years."

Dunlap and his associates at the Sea Museum eventually found the lens at the Mystic Seaport Museum in Connecticut, which had never managed to raise the money necessary to restore it. "We asked the Coast Guard to give it back to us so we could restore it and display it," says Dunlap. "They agreed."

However, after more than sixty years in storage, the lens was in terrible shape. "All the glazing had fallen out, the glass was loose, and there was no hardware, no framework," says Dunlap. What was worse, many of the delicate glass prisms were broken or missing. "There's some pretty severe breakage," says Dunlap. "That's a big problem because the glass can be reproduced, but it's a very expensive process."

In fact, the cost of repairing damaged Fresnels can run to a million dollars or more, a price beyond the reach of most exhibitors. Nor can the U.S. Coast Guard afford to rescue its own damaged lenses. As a result, many of these unique and historic devices have been discarded or sold, and many others remain in crates because no one can afford to restore them. It is all part of what Dunlap describes as the "tragedy of the Fresnels."

A staircase of more than 200 steps spirals inside the 175-foot tower of the **Ponce de Leon Inlet Lighthouse.**

Lens Doctor Makes a House Call

"The tragedy started when they electrified the lights," says Dunlap. "All of a sudden they didn't need quite as many keepers at each light station. The lights were a lot easier to take care of because the keepers weren't up there constantly cleaning soot off the glass. So the lenses didn't get the tender loving care they had when there was a full complement of keepers at each light station. Later it got to the point where the Coast Guard could simply send a team over every three or four months to change the bulbs and so on. So many of the Fresnel lenses still in use today are suffering."

However, a new and innovative process is causing lighthouse museums to take a new look at broken Fresnels previously thought irreparable. Soon, it may be possible to bring these magnificent old lenses back to life. Damaged panels are being replaced with molded acrylic prisms that look and function like the originals. Mechanical designer Dan Spinella pioneered the technique, and now he is working with Dunlap and his associates at Ponce de Leon Inlet to help restore the station's original lens.

Although he had no previous experience in optics, Spinella became interested in the subject during the early 1990s when asked to help with restoration of the first-order lens at St. Augustine. "There were fourteen damaged prisms that needed to be replaced. The cost would have been $55,000, the equivalent of about $4,000 per prism."

Spinella felt this nearly prohibitive cost could be reduced. "I did a lot of research at the National Archives and maritime research centers and societies and was able to come up with drawings and formulas."

Dan Spinella

The prisms of **Fresnel lenses** like this one now on display at the Sea Museum in Ponce Inlet, Florida, focus light into a powerful beam.

To painstakingly shape a block of glass following the original French designs would have been far too expensive. So Spinella started looking for another suitable material, one that could be molded instead. "I came up with acrylic," he says. "It has the same index of refraction as the crown glass used to make Fresnels in the 1800s."

Spinella found that the finished acrylic prisms behaved exactly like glass. When a special green pigment was added to the plastic, they even had the light-green tint of the originals. But they were far less costly. They could be produced for about $400, or ten percent of the original $4,000 estimates for grinding and polishing glass prisms.

"This makes restorations more feasible," says the modest Spinella.

No doubt, Augustine Fresnel would have been impressed by this lens doctor's accomplishment.

Many lighthouses still use the prismatic lenses developed by French inventor Augustine Fresnel during the 1820s. Today, the carefully shaped and polished glass prisms are very difficult and expensive to reproduce.

Seminoles Burn White Man's Totem

B uilt on Key Biscayne in 1821, not long after the United States acquired Florida from the Spanish, the Cape Florida Lighthouse guards the nation's strategic southeastern corner. During the 1820s and afterward, the flow of ships traveling from New Orleans or the Caribbean toward the bustling ports of the eastern seaboard increased dramatically. The beacon calling to these vessels from the cape was their visual anchor.

The journey through the Florida Keys and around the cape was a dangerous one. Mariners in these waters were threatened by reefs, hurricanes, and pirates. Meanwhile, the lighthouse had problems of its own. The hostile Seminoles in southern Florida had come to view it as a symbol of the hated white man's power.

"The sight of the lighthouse on what they considered to be hallowed ground really upset them," explains author and historian Joan Gill Blank, a forty-five-year resident of Key Biscayne. "It signified the U.S. presence here. To them this had become the white man's totem."

The lighthouse had operated in relative peace for almost fifteen years by 1836, when war broke out between white settlers and the Seminoles. Among the first targets of Seminole war parties was the lighthouse. "In mid-afternoon on July 23, 1836, approximately forty warriors came up through the mangroves," says Blank. "They had their war paint on, and they were carrying their rifles."

Keeper John W. Thompson and his assistant spotted the attackers and took refuge in the tower, locking the heavy wooden door behind them. Armed with three muskets and a barrel of gunpowder, they managed to hold off the warriors for a time, but soon fire arrows set the tower ablaze. Driven up the wooden steps by the flames, the two keepers made their last stand in the lantern room. The assistant was finally cut down by shots from below, but Thompson, although he was practically roasted alive by the inferno, managed to hold on. Wounded several times and badly burned, he was nonetheless still alive the next day when the *Motto*, a U.S. Navy warship, came to his rescue.

With the tower steps burned away, the *Motto*'s shore party had to find a way to get Thompson down from the top of the ninety-five-foot tower. "They tried to send a kite up, but it did not work," says Blank. "Finally, two sailors scaled the tower, rigged up something similar to a boson's chair, and lowered him to the ground."

The **Cape Florida Lighthouse** as it looked before a recent restoration. The weathered courses of brick shown here have been patched and the tower given a gleaming white coat of paint.

Jack McDonald

The restored **Cape Florida Light** is now a popular attraction, thanks to the fund-raising efforts of the Dade County Heritage Trust.

Thompson eventually recovered from his wounds. The lighthouse itself almost did not. The Seminole threat made it impossible to make repairs for nearly ten years. But, having survived the fire and a decade of neglect, the hollow-walled brick tower remained solid. It was restored and back in operation by 1846.

In 1878, just thirty-two years later, its light was extinguished again—this time by the Lighthouse Service. Completion of the Fowey Rocks Lighthouse on an open-water reef about ten miles south of the cape had made the light obsolete. Afterward, the Cape Florida tower stood dark for almost 120 years, more than twice as long as it had served as an active aid to navigation. Recently, however, this national treasure and Florida landmark has been handsomely refurbished with funds raised by the Dade County Heritage Trust. The tower now sports a fresh coat of stucco and white paint. Its lamp was relit in 1996 during the Miami Centennial celebration. The lighthouse is now open to the public as part of the Bill Bagg's Cape Florida State Recreation Area.

Last Stand at Key West

A century after keeper Thompson used the Cape Florida light tower as his last redoubt, the old U.S. Lighthouse Service made its own last stand at Key West. The Service, which had guided mariners and served the nation for 140 years, had its final say, symbolically at least, in a jowl-to-jowl shouting match between President Franklin Delano Roosevelt and Key West Lighthouse keeper William McDemeritt in 1939.

Key West has known a lot of conflict in the past, but most of it has been between nature and the people who have tried to make a life here. Located more than a hundred miles from the mainland at the end of the long chain of low sandy islands and reefs known as the Florida Keys, Key West has been the target for countless gales and hurricanes. The town, known for its margaritas and easygoing lifestyle, was once the home of pirates and wreckers who made a living salvaging ships that had been broken to pieces by the deadly Florida Reef.

The Keys and their reefs comprise what may be the most dangerous navigational obstacle on the planet. Since the 1500s, when entire Spanish treasure fleets were lost here, thousands of ships have met disaster in the Keys. Salvaging their cargoes

The delicate-looking **Sand Key Lighthouse** has saved countless ships from running aground on the almost invisible islet located about seven miles southwest of Key West.

Jack McDonald

A $500,000 restoration project in the late 1980s left the **Key West Lighthouse** in pristine condition.

became a lucrative industry and Key West its home port.

During the 1820s, the navy established a base at Key West and set about the task of flushing pirates from the Keys and regulating the often questionable activities of the wreckers. By 1825 a lighthouse was guiding naval warships in and out of the harbor. Destroyed by a hurricane in 1847, it was replaced by a taller tower located some distance inland from the original. The new station eventually received a third-order Fresnel lens and was raised to a height of eighty-six feet.

William McDemeritt became keeper of the Key West Light in 1917. By 1939, when President Roosevelt's visit was announced, McDemeritt had served at this post for twenty-two years. He was also commander of the Seventh Lighthouse District and had more than 800 employees and $15 million worth of federal property under his control. He was a man of some substance. "And [he] was quite a character," says Joe Pais, assistant director of the Key West Art and Historical Society. "He built aviaries where he kept exotic birds and made the place look like a tropical garden."

But the life McDemeritt had built for himself was about to change dramatically. The Lighthouse Service itself was about to disappear, and with it, McDemeritt's job. President Roosevelt had ordered the Coast Guard to take responsibility for all U.S. navigational aids, including lighthouses. The Lighthouse Service, one of the government's oldest and most efficiently run agencies would be closed down. Some historians believe Roosevelt made this move to help bolster the nation's defenses in advance of World War II. For a man such as McDemeritt, however, the decision was an outrage, whatever the president's reasons for it.

"He was a very independent man," says Pais, "but I think he was smart enough with his engineering background to know that the time of the lighthouse keeper was coming to an end."

When Roosevelt arrived in Key West, McDemeritt confronted him. "There was the president in his open car, with his cigarette sticking out," says Pais. "He was being introduced to the local dignitaries and, of course, William McDemeritt was one of them."

McDemeritt stepped up to the president's touring car and told him face to face what he thought of the decision to close down the Lighthouse Service. Roosevelt, never at a loss for words, fired back. "I'm sure Mr. Roosevelt told him to step back and do what he was supposed to do as a government employee," says Pais. "Mr. McDemeritt responded in an arrogant fashion, and a heated confrontation ensued."

A photographer caught the two men growling at one another. The picture of Roosevelt with his fist raised and McDemeritt leaning angrily toward him in his fedora is a favorite of Pais's. "I'm sure, if the president could have reached out and grabbed him by the throat, he would have, and there would have been some real fisticuffs," says Pais.

Ultimately, McDemeritt did lose his job, but not because he had argued with the president. Care of the nation's lighthouses was placed in the hands of the Coast Guard, and the Lighthouse Service ceased to exist. Lighthouse Service personnel were allowed to transfer into the Coast Guard, but McDemeritt chose not to do so.

McDemeritt's independent spirit can still be seen and felt all over Key West. "We're out here on our own," says Pais. "We're on an island 104 miles from the mainland and 156 miles from Miami. We're actually closer to Cuba, which is only 90 miles away. So we are very independent people."

Each April, Key West declares its independence in a water-and-alcohol-soaked celebration of the "Conch Republic." During the celebration, Key West is no longer considered sovereign U.S. territory—at least that is what the participants say. The Conch Republic is more or less a mythical entity, but according to Pais, some Key West businesses have taken to flying the banner of the Republic instead of the American flag. Not surprisingly, the banner is emblazoned with a conch shell. Maybe there should be a lighthouse on the banner instead.

With the exception of the traditional brick tower on Key West, the lighthouses of the Florida Keys are unlike any others in America. The North American continent is making a geological last stand here and there is little solid ground on which to construct towers. As a result, the lighthouses at Sand Key, Sombrero Key, American Shoal, Alligator Shoal, Carysfort Reef, and Fowey Rocks all stand in open water. Building them presented the Lighthouse Service with a special challenge, but nineteenth-century technology proved up to the task. The cast-iron and steel towers were anchored to piles driven deep into the sands and underlying coral. Their open, skeleton-style structures allowed even hurricane-force winds to pass through while doing little damage. As a result, these extraordinary reef lighthouse, built between 1852 and 1880, still stand today after almost one and a half centuries. While none of the reef lighthouses are open to the public, they can be seen and enjoyed from the Overseas Highway (U.S. 1) linking Key West with the mainland.

St. George Ree

Battery Point

Trinidad Hea

Old Table Bluff L

Poi

CALIFORNIA

Lights of the
Golden Coast

City

orial Light in Trinidad (replica)

locino Light

.Fort Bragg

ht

.Santa Rosa

East Brother Light
Point Reyes Light
Alcatraz Light
Point Bonita Light Yerba Buena Light
Fort Point Light
.Oakland
San Francisco

Point Montara Light

.San Jose
Pigeon Point Light

Monterey
Bay
Point Pinos Light
Monterey

Point Sur Light
.Big Sur

.San Simeon

Point Hueneme Light .Oxnard

Los Angeles .

Point Vincente Light
Point Fermin Light

Old Point Loma Light .San Diego
Point Loma Light

Dragon Rocks

California is where the West ends. This is true in both a physical and legendary sense, for only a few miles beyond the San Andreas fault, the migrations of a continent and a people reach their outer limits. Here a wall of desert mountains drops down into the sea, and except for a scatter of islands, there is no more solid ground for at least another five thousand miles.

Battery Point Light

Approximately one out of every ten Americans lives in California, and the rest of us—whether we are willing to admit it or not—would like to visit. California is a sort of grail for Americans, and at least once in our lives, we all reach for it. Strangely enough, when we get there and stand gazing out at the ocean from Point Loma, near San Diego, Point Reyes, near San Francisco, or Battery Point, near Crescent City in the far north, we secretly wish we could keep on going. But we can't. We bump up against, or splash into, the Pacific Ocean. Most of the time, it is cold and rough, so we have to stop.

Perhaps that is why lighthouses make such perfect symbols for California. Their beacons stretch far out over the blue horizon to places we can only reach in our dreams. In this way lighthouses are the essence of this magical state. And for this reason a tour of California lights can be both a great vacation and a spiritual adventure.

The following is just such a lighthouse tour. It is a difficult journey to duplicate on your own, especially if you try to do the whole thing all at once. More than eight-hundred miles of winding road lie between Crescent City and San Diego. That is a long drive, and you will have to take a few boats, ferries, or small airplanes along the way. We suggest, for the moment at least, you relax and enjoy the ride as you travel along with us.

We begin our journey on a wave-swept pinnacle of rock about six miles off the extreme northern coast of California. While it is not the westernmost point in California—that honor goes to Cape Mendocino a hundred miles or so to the south—you really can't get much farther out than St. George Reef. This place is almost out of sight from the mainland, and of course, you have to take a boat or helicopter to get here.

St. George Reef was once known as Dragon Rock, perhaps because it blasted so many ships and destroyed so many lives. The rock was born in fire—the dragon's breath. It is the peak of a mountain of basaltic rock created long ago by volcanic forces deep in the earth. With no surrounding shallows, it rises abruptly from the ocean floor to a point just above the surface.

The passengers and crew of the side-wheeler *Brother Jonathan* must have thought the rock a killer dragon when it tore open the wooden hull of their vessel in 1865. The fatally stricken *Brother Jonathan* sank in minutes, and more than two hundred lives were lost. But despite this tragedy and others that followed, the rock was not marked with a lighthouse until 1892. Anyone who has watched storm-driven waves explode when they hit the rock can readily understand the delay. Most federal officials thought it impossible to build a lighthouse in this exposed place, but there were some who believed it could be done. In time, mariners began to call the rock St. George Reef, perhaps in hopes the dragon would eventually be slain.

Finally, under pressure from the public and maritime interests anxious to avoid more losses of ships and lives, the government decided to attempt construction of a light station on St. George Reef. In 1882 the project finally got started, but it proved an arduous—probably it is better described as heroic—undertaking. For month after month, year after year, workmen shuttled back and forth to the rock from a tender anchored nearby. First they built an enormous, elliptical concrete platform. Then, atop this massive base they erected a hulking, granite tower consisting of 1,339 huge blocks. Finally, in the lantern room, more than 140 feet above the waves, they installed the finest available first-order Fresnel lens. In all, construction of the St. George Reef Station took more than ten years, and it cost the U.S. government $704,633, in nineteenth-century dollars, making it the most expensive lighthouse in the nation's history.

Courtesy National Archives

Constantly challenged by Pacific waves, the **St. George Lighthouse** marks a collection of exposed rocks and ledges—the summit of an underwater mountain. Keepers lived at this isolated station from 1892 until 1975, when the Coast Guard abandoned it.

First lit on the evening of October 20, 1892, the light would serve for the better part of a century. Since families were never housed at this isolated and dangerous station, it was maintained by an all-male crew. Forced by their duties to live here for months at a time, the lonely keepers found the tower damp, cold, and uncomfortable. Most considered the St. George Reef Station an unpleasant and undesirable posting. No doubt to the relief of its Coast Guard crewmen, the lighthouse was abandoned in 1975 and its job of marking the reef taken over by a large, untended buoy.

Although the St. George Reef Lighthouse was never very popular with keepers, it now fascinates the public. Tourists with binoculars gather along Washington Boulevard in Crescent City hoping for a glimpse of the historic structure. Thanks to Guy Towers, Bob Bolen, and other preservationists, people may soon get a much closer look. Towers and Bolen have been working together since the late 1980s to save the lighthouse and restore it, with the intention of opening it to the public.

Guy Towers

Towers traces his interest in lighthouses to a backpacking trip through a wild stretch of the California coast where he came across the abandoned Punta Gorda Light Station. He wondered what had happened to this old lighthouse. Why had it been closed? What had it been like to serve there as a keeper? Afterward, Towers began to research the history of California lighthouses. Then, when he moved to Crescent City in 1986, he encountered the St. George Reef Lighthouse.

"It was like greeting an old friend," recalls Towers. "And it occurred to me that here was the Mount Everest of lighthouses."

Towers felt that something

Bob Bolen

should be done to preserve this historic treasure. So he contacted Bob Bolen, who was trying to acquire the station's first-order classical lens. Since the federal government had put the lighthouse up for sale, the two men realized that time could be running out.

"We set up interpretive displays all over Crescent City," says Towers. "We raised public awareness anyway we could and worked our way through scores of government agencies."

Just as construction of the station had taken ten years, so too did the effort to save it. But by the mid-1990s, Towers and Bolen had convinced the government to place the lighthouse in their care as part of a long-term lease agreement. Now they are trying to restore it, a process they know will take many more years and a lot of money and hard work.

Twenty years of neglect have left many scars. Paint has peeled, plaster has fallen, and flooring has crumbled. Glass in the lantern room has been shattered by storm winds and bullets fired by thoughtless pleasure boaters who sometimes use the tower for target practice.

"It's a big task and will take a long time, but somebody has to do it," says Bolen. "You have to start someplace."

Bolen's personal interest in St. George Reef reaches back to his childhood. "When I grew up here during the Depression, the St. George Reef Lighthouse was a mystery. It was off-limits, and being off-limits, it always fascinated me. It was the other side of the world as far as I was concerned. I never dreamed that I would ever get out here. But here I am standing in this jewel of a lighthouse."

You Really Live Here?

With its clapboard houses and Victorian inns, Crescent City has an old-fashioned, small-town atmosphere. It is somewhat surprising that federal officials thought the place important enough to mark with one of the West's earliest lighthouses, but they did indeed. During the 1850s, this far-northern California port was the most important lumbering center on the Pacific coast. Redwood beams and planks shipped from Crescent City made possible the construction of old San Francisco.

Built in 1856 on Battery Point near the entrance to the Crescent City harbor, the lighthouse consisted of a simple Cape Cod–style dwelling with a tower rising through the center of the roof. Its beacon was focused by a fourth-order Fresnel lens imported from France. The story of this station would be no more or less remarkable than that of other early California lighthouses except for the fact that the original structure still stands little changed in more than 140 years. Its thick stone walls have outlasted several generations of keepers.

Although the light was discontinued in 1965, it was re-established in 1982 as a private aid to navigation. Owned by the Del Norte County Historical Society, the lighthouse is now a museum. Unlike most navigational museums, however, this one has full-time residents. The venerable lighthouse is home to Don and Carol Vestal, who serve as tour guides as well as the station's keepers.

Don Vestal

Decorated with Christmas lights, the **Battery Point Lighthouse** near Crescent City competes with a California sunset. Among the oldest light stations in the West, this combination dwelling and tower has served since 1856.

"Being a modern-day lighthouse keeper doesn't involve as many chores as the old-time keepers did," says Don Vestal. "Mostly we meet people and deal with the public."

Living in the lighthouse and maintaining it are also part of the Vestal's duties. "Some people don't believe we live here," says Don Vestal. "They ask us 'Do you really live in the lighthouse?' and I tell them, 'Yep, that's my side of the bed and that's my teddy bear.'"

Visitors find the history of the lighthouse fascinating. They want to know who lived here a century ago and what life was like for early keepers. The Vestals are happy to share what they have learned of the station's past.

"Living here gives you a lot of respect for the keepers and their wives," says Carol Vestal. "In this lighthouse the wife served as the assistant keeper."

Many of the keepers here had children, and they, too, helped keep the light burning. "The whole family pitched in," says Don Vestal. "Even the little kids helped. And there was plenty to do."

Carol Vestal

While the Vestals' duties are not the same as those of traditional keepers, they manage to stay plenty busy. More than ten thousand people tour the lighthouse each year, and it can get crowded on Battery Point, especially during the summer tourist season. But the Vestals feel that the rewards of their work far outweigh the long hours and occasional lack of privacy.

"When the tide comes in and nobody is on the island, then it's all ours," says Don Vestal. "Usually, we sit outside and watch the sunset. Then we come inside, light the candles, play the Victrola with the old records, and just enjoy being alone in such a historic building."

"It's like living a fantasy," says Carol Vestal.

A Hard Reality

Despite the romantic view of lighthouses now shared by nearly everyone, life at the often remote stations could be very hard—and dangerous. Sudden storms, high winds, and pounding waves were a constant threat. In 1914 a tidal wave of stupendous height and power almost carried away the little lighthouse on Trinidad Head, about fifty miles south of Crescent City. Although the station's squat tower was perched on top of a two-hundred-foot cliff, the huge wave swept right over it. Inside the tower keeper Fred Harrington was knocked off his feet and, with green water swirling all around him, hung on for dear life. Although the lantern room windows were shattered and lamps and machinery damaged, Harrington had the light burning again within thirty minutes.

Cape Mendocino Light

Built in 1871, the Trinidad Head Lighthouse survived this and many other near calamities. It still stands today, its automated beacon guiding fishing boats in and out of the harbor at bucolic Trinidad. The station is closed to the public and difficult to see from the town or nearby Highway 101. Easier to reach is a replica of the tower built as a memorial to local sailors who have lost their lives to the sea. The replica is located on Trinity Street and overlooks the town's scenic harbor, which in summer is filled with fishing boats and pleasure craft. Some Trinidad fishermen sell fresh salmon and other ocean delights from their garages or front yards.

Waves and water were also a problem at the Humboldt Bay Lighthouse near Eureka. Completed in 1856, the station was hit repeatedly by storms and earthquakes, which eventually left it a shambles. When gales pushed unusually high tides into the bay, the residence was completely awash. In 1892 the keepers were transferred to a new lighthouse on Table Bluff, and no doubt, they were happy to go. In time the old station was undercut by erosion and tumbled down into a pile of rubble on the beach.

Years later, the Table Bluff Lighthouse would also be threatened with destruction. Decommissioned by the Coast Guard in 1975, it fell into disrepair and might have been torn down except for the intervention of preservationist Ray Glavich. With the help of local volunteers, he repaired the square, wooden tower and had it trucked off to Woodley Island Marina in Eureka, where it now serves as a reminder of the region's rich maritime heritage.

"Lighthouses like this one played an important role in the history of this bay," says Glavich. "And, that history is still being written."

The history of the Cape Mendocino Lighthouse already has been written—or most of it, anyway. Cape Mendocino's soaring cliffs drop almost vertically into the Pacific and form one of the West's most imposing headlands. A squat, twenty-foot-tall light tower built with great difficulty on the side of the cliffs in 1868 took advantage of a four-hundred-foot elevation to cast its beacon more than twenty-five miles out to sea. During the 1950s, after serving mariners for more than eighty years, its first-order Fresnel lens was removed and the station all but abandoned. Nowadays, a rather unromantic pole light guards the cape, and all the original station structures are either gone or fallen into ruin.

During its active years, the Cape Mendocino Lighthouse was one of the most remote and uncomfortable navigational stations in the country. Supplies were brought in irregularly by tenders and hauled up the steep slopes to the lighthouse. Nearly every day fierce winds shook the walls and made life miserable for the crew. The station is said to be haunted, if not by the ghosts of its hard-living keepers, then at least by memories of the dedicated work they did here.

Looking Past the Rust

Unlike the light station on rugged Cape Mendocino, the Point Cabrillo Lighthouse about a hundred miles down the coast was considered a highly desirable duty station by most keepers, especially those with families. Ready access to stores, churches, and schools in the nearby town of Mendocino made living relatively easy here.

"Even so, these people worked their tails off," says Lisa Weg, manager of the Point Cabrillo Lighthouse, now maintained by the California Coast Conservancy.

The keeper's hard daily and nightly routines were much the same at Point Cabrillo as at other light stations along the coast. The beacon, established in 1909, had to be kept in operation. The buildings and machinery had to be maintained in top condition.

Point Cabrillo Light

During the 1970s, the station was automated, and the last keepers packed their bags and moved elsewhere. Replaced by an airport-style beacon, the third-order Fresnel lens was neglected, and station structures were allowed to deteriorate. Eventually, the lighthouse property and surrounding acreage were targeted for development.

"This would have been a development of fifty-five new homes" says Weg. "But there was a lot of concern in the community about saving this last bit of undeveloped coastline and saving the light station."

Funds raised under the auspices of the California Coastal Conservancy have changed the destiny of the lighthouse and its pastoral setting. No homes will be built here. Instead, the station will be restored and become the prime attraction of a public park. It will have much to offer visitors interested in lighthouse history and in a way of life that vanished with the closing of America's last manned light stations.

"One of the special things about this place is that you can walk down here and see what a turn-of-the-century lighthouse was like," says Weg. "The lighthouse is little changed, that is, if you can look past the rust. The property around the station looks much as it did when keepers ran their cattle and sheep and raised potatoes here."

Lisa Weg

Weg is researching the lives of Point Cabrillo keepers. "One of things I've most enjoyed about my job is searching out the children of keepers and getting them to talk about their family histories," says Weg. "For them and for us, lighthouses remain both a warning beacon and a guidepost. I guess we all need a little of that in our lives."

Blanket of Memories

The San Andreas Fault runs directly under the Point Arena Lighthouse, plunging into the sea just north of the tower. A million years of earthquakes and of continental plates grinding past one another have torn asunder the Point Arena cliffs, leaving jagged rocks to crush the hulls of ships that stray too close. But while the point bares its teeth to mariners, it turns a far more hospitable face to those who come by land. Just ask the Owens sisters. They grew up here during the late 1930s and 1940s when their father, William Owens, was keeper of the Point Arena Lighthouse.

The Owens sisters

"When I look back on it, I'd say we had a very good life," says Shirley Stormes, one of William Owens's six daughters. "I wish somehow I could get back to it."

Now Stormes has returned to Point Arena for a brief visit in the company of her sisters, Diana Brown and Sarah Swartz. It has been almost half a century since they lived in the keeper's residence and played in the fields and streams surrounding the station.

"We had no television," says Stormes. "We had a radio that we listened to once in a while and we heard *Inner Sanctum* and such. But we spent most of our time outside. I remember we were playing outside on the day the war broke out and Dad called us in to listen to the news about Pearl Harbor."

To the sisters, the violence of the war seemed very distant from idyllic Point Arena. "We kind of took care of ourselves and made our own fun," says Swartz. "Yes, we made our own fun. We did then, and we still do today."

"All of us were loners," remarks Brown. "We're still loners. We don't like to be in the city and in crowds."

"That's right, we are loners," chimes in Stormes. "We don't like a lot of people around us."

California's San Andreas Fault created these threatening cliffs and jagged rocks. Since 1870, the **Point Arena Light** has warned ships to keep away.

The Owens sisters take considerable comfort in memories of their childhood at Point Arena. "When the fog came in, I used to love to sit in front of the fireplace," says Stormes. "With the white all around, it was just like being covered by a blanket."

"Even the light coming through the bedroom window could be comforting," says Brown.

The sisters say that, as children, they gave little thought to the comfort the Point Arena Light provided to others. "My dad taught us to turn the light on," says Swartz. "We had to do that, but it was just a job to us. We never thought about what it was doing for the ships. It was just our life."

It was a life the sisters say they would like to live once more, perhaps in a lighthouse like the one at Point Arena. "I guess we're going to hit the lottery, buy a lighthouse, and all go and live in it," says Swartz.

The sisters agree in chorus. "Wouldn't that be wonderful!"

Only forty feet tall, this squat tower marks **Point Reyes,** one of the West's most dangerous navigational obstacles. The towering cliffs give the tower a mighty boost so that its light shines out to sea from an elevation of almost 300 feet. The station's huge first-order Fresnel lens remains in place.

A Tunnel in Time

Of course, not all lighthouse experiences were so dreamy as those remembered and treasured by the Owens sisters. Some keepers found the isolation and punishing weather oppressive. A late-nineteenth-century keeper at the Point Reyes Lighthouse northwest of San Francisco made the following desperate log entry: "Solitude, where are your charms? Better dwell in the midst of alarms than in this horrible place."

Socked in by fog approximately 110 days a year, Point Reyes must have seemed a very lonely and melancholy place to keepers who served here one after another for more than a century. Clinging to a cliff 250 feet above the Pacific, the station could hardly have been more isolated. Established in 1870, the lighthouse was not automated until 1975, probably because its beacon was considered so important.

This light warns mariners away from what many consider to be the West's most dangerous navigational obstacle. The rocky shores of Point Reyes reach fifteen miles out into the ocean, all but blocking one of the primary shipping channels leading to San Francisco. The formidable blade of Point Reyes has been ripping open the hulls of ships since the sixteenth century, and literally hundreds of large vessels have been lost to its merciless rocks. No one will ever know how many other, more fortunate ships have been saved by the Point Reyes Lighthouse.

While the light station remains in operation, it is now part of the Point Reyes National Seashore, a popular attraction for those who love nature and spectacular ocean scenery. Visitors often stop at the lighthouse to enjoy the extraordinary view and learn about the point's turbulent history. Occasionally, seashore ranger Bryan Aptekar leads evening lighthouse tours and invites visitors to go with him through what he describes as a "time tunnel." At

Bryan Aptekar

night, the steep, three-hundred-foot climb down to the light tower makes it easy to imagine one is a nineteenth-century Point Reyes keeper descending the stairs to check the light.

"If you don't have a flashlight, make friends with someone who does," Aptekar tells his tour groups. Then slowly and carefully he shepherds them through the darkness and down the 308 steps to the tower. "Imagine as we go down the stairs tonight that this is a time tunnel," he says. "You are going back in time to 1870, when this lighthouse was first built."

Once inside the lighthouse Aptekar shows off its antique equipment. Nowadays, the Point Reyes beacon shines from a modern plastic optic mounted on top of the nearby fog-signal building, but for more than a century the light was focused by an enormous first-order Fresnel lens. For historical reasons the big classical lens has been left in the lantern room. Aptekar explains how heavy machinery was used to rotate the lens and make its light appear to flash.

'The whole six-thousand-pound lens spun around on these little chariot wheels," he says "The twenty-four vertical glass panels you see here focused the light into separate beams like the spokes of a giant wagon wheel. As the lens turned, the light appeared to flash, once every five seconds."

Aptekar makes it clear that the keepers who maintained the light were a hardy breed. "This is the windiest place on the West Coast," he says. "It is also the foggiest place on the West Coast. We can have a whole week of fog when you can't see twenty feet in front of you. Sometimes, because of the wind and fog, the keepers had to crawl back up the steps from the tower. But whatever the conditions, the keeper and his assistants had to run this place twenty-four hours a day. It was an endless job, a monotonous job with no weekends or holidays."

Light on the Birdman's Island

On occasion, keepers at Point Reyes and other remote light stations must have felt shut in and cut off from the world by the weather and isolation. But the keepers of the West's oldest light station were constantly reminded of a much harsher variety of confinement. For many years, they lived and worked right next door to the nation's most notorious maximum security lockup.

Established in 1854, the Alcatraz Island Lighthouse was the first major navigational station in the West. Like other early Western lights, it owed its existence to the California Gold Rush.

"In January of 1848 gold was discovered and the world rushed into San Francisco," says John Martini, who serves as historian for the Golden Gate National Recreation Area. "Ships were coming in here and their crews jumping ship and running off to the gold fields."

John Martini

The mighty influx of ships and prospectors drawn to California by gold fever caught the U.S. government by surprise—and woefully unprepared. Hundreds of ships set sail for San Francisco, and half of them wrecked before ever reaching port. To save lives and deal with the extraordinary increase in shipping, Congress launched a crash lighthouse construction program.

"Early on Alcatraz Island was recognized as a hazard to navigation," says Martini. "All shipping in and out of the harbor had to go around the rock. In many unfortunate cases, they hit it. So priority was given to this giant obstacle sitting right here in the middle of San Francisco Bay."

Hired by the government to build eight West Coast lighthouses, Baltimore contractor Francis Gibbons began his Olympian task by erecting a small, Cape Cod–style combination tower and dwelling on Alcatraz Island. The station was completed and in operation by the summer of 1854.

"Simultaneously, the U.S. Army fortified the island with hundreds of gun emplacements," says Martini. "This was to protect the ships and fight off any bad guys who might want to take over San Francisco."

Eventually, the island would be used to keep bad guys in rather than drive them away. For more than fifty years, the light station shared its rocky roost with military and civilian prisons, but it was the federal penitentiary established here in 1934 that forever gave the name Alcatraz its cold and forbidding ring. The steel doors of the federal pen, known to most of its inmates only as "the Rock," slammed shut on Al Capone and many other hardened criminals. Also incarcerated here for several years was Robert Stroud, the ornithologist who came to be called the "Birdman of Alcatraz."

The light tower seen on Alcatraz Island today is not the original. All but destroyed by the great San Francisco earthquake of 1906, the structure Gibbons had built was soon torn down to make way for a maximum security prison. In 1909 it was replaced by a reinforced concrete tower and adjacent bay-style dwelling. The height of the eighty-four-foot octagonal tower allowed its light to be seen even above the high walls of the prison. The light was automated in 1963 at about the same time the penitentiary was closed. The two-story keepers dwelling burned in 1969, but the tower remains standing. It is seen by many as a symbol for the bay and the city of San Francisco. Tour boats docked near Fisherman's Wharf offer tours of the island, prison, and lighthouse.

The End of America

To reach the San Francisco Bay, ships must pass through the narrow and often treacherous Golden Gate Straits. Since 1855 a beacon shining from rugged Point Bonita has shown the way. Built in 1855, not long after the light station on Alcatraz Island was completed, the original Point Bonita Lighthouse stood on a high ledge more than three hundred feet above the sea. It was, in fact, so far above the water that low-lying clouds and fog often made its light invisible to ships tossing in the waves below. To fix this problem a second lighthouse was built down closer to the water where its beacon would be more effective. Completed and in service by 1877, the new thirty-three-foot tower stood on a frightfully narrow ledge 124 feet above the water.

"It's not the biggest lighthouse on the California coast," says Martini, "and not the oldest, but it sure is the most dramatic."

The tower's perch is a precarious one and over the years much of the land around it has broken away from the cliffs and tumbled into the ocean. Waves pound the rocks on three

sides of the station, and the tower can be reached only via a lengthy wooden suspension bridge.

"The ocean, the wind, the waves, erosion—those are the powers in charge here," says Martini.

Because Point Bonita is an exposed and dangerous place, the lighthouse is not generally open to the public. However, the Golden Gate National Recreation Area offers a variety of daylight and evening tours.

"Some lighthouses really speak to you because of their location, and this one certainly does," says Martini. "When you walk out to Point Bonita, you feel like you are going as far out as you can go and still be on this continent. This is the end of America."

Point Bonita Lighthouse clings precariously to a cliff near San Francisco.

Bed, Breakfast, and Fog Signal

Once they passed through the Golden Gate Strait and got safely around Alcatraz Island, seamen still faced many challenges. Most of the San Francisco Bay was dangerously shallow, and there were many threatening shoals. Several lighthouses helped ships' pilots pick their way through the narrow navigable channels. One of these was located on Yerba Buena Island, also known as Goat Island, near where the San Francisco–Oakland Bridge now crosses the bay. Its light guided ferries and marked a small harbor where lightships and lighthouse tenders were berthed.

The **East Brother Lighthouse** in San Francisco Bay glows romantically at dusk. The station is now an attractive bed-and-breakfast inn.

Walter Fanning was born at the Yerba Buena Lighthouse in 1909. While his father, a sailor in the U.S. Navy, was away at sea, his mother lived with her parents at the lighthouse. Fanning's grandfather served as assistant keeper at Yerba Buena and later as head keeper at the East Brother Island Lighthouse farther up the bay. Fanning did much of his growing up at the two light stations.

Fanning has especially fond memories of the East Brother Island Station. "There was good fishing there," he says. "We caught striped bass and rock cod."

When not fishing or cleaning his catch, Fanning had the run of the Station. "The place was particularly interesting in the fog," he says "They had big, ten-inch brass fog whistles on the roof, and the engine room was steamy and warm and smelled of hot oil."

Walter Fanning

The Yerba Buena Lighthouse survived automation and the end of the era of manned light stations. Today, its original fourth-order Fresnel lens still shines from the two-story octagonal tower. A Coast Guard admiral lives in the keeper's dwelling where Fanning was born.

The lighthouse on East Brother Island, however, was very nearly torn down when its beacon was automated in 1967. Built in 1874, Victorian-style combination tower and dwelling marked the passage linking San Francisco Bay with the smaller San Pablo Bay to the north. Then, during the 1960s, the Coast Guard removed the station's crew and announced plans to raze the building. One of those who stepped in to save the venerable structure was Walter Fanning.

"A group of us protested so loudly that the Coast Guard said, in effect, 'if you love this place so much, you take it,' " says Fanning. "So we did."

It took more than ten years to organize the support and raise the money needed to restore the lighthouse to its former glory. "We started in February 1980," says Fanning. "On weekends we had as many as twenty people out here working. We took our woodworking machines out there and rebuilt the Victorian scrolls and scrimshaw. We reconditioned the fog signal and got it working again. By October it was all done."

Once restored, the East Brother Island Lighthouse began a new career as a bed-and-breakfast inn. Surrounded by the waters of the bay, the inn can only be reached by boat, and this makes staying here a particularly romantic experience. In addition to enjoying some of California's finest sunsets, guests can watch ships moving into San Pablo Bay and onward into the Sacramento River. In the evening they can climb the tower and imagine themselves to be keepers of the light. In a way, they actually are keepers since proceeds go toward upkeep of the historic station.

Lighthouse Hostel

Travelers who would like to stay at an authentic California light station have another option at Point Montara on the west side of the San Francisco Peninsula. The Point Montara Lighthouse is available to overnight guests as a low-cost hostel.

"We are open to recreational travelers," says Rich Lilley, who manages the facility. "We provide family or dorm-style accommodations, kitchens, laundry, telephone, and a nice shared experience for everyone."

An important part of what people share here is the lighthouse itself. Shining from a short, cast-iron tower positioned at the edge of a cliff,

Rich Lilley

the beacon remains in operation. The existing structure was built in 1928, when it replaced an earlier wooden tower. The fog signal now sounds from a buoy rolling in the Pacific waves some distance out from shore.

Lilley knows the station well. He has been manager here since the hostel opened in 1980. "We were the first to use a historical lighthouse as a hostel," he says.

Hostel guests can enjoy a wide range of activities. "We have whale watching, fishing, hiking, sea kayaking, and surfing to enjoy," says Lilley. "And we have the ocean environment. It's an exciting place."

For nearly three decades **Point Montara** had only a fog signal to warn sailors of its jagged rocks, but in 1900 a lighthouse was added. The light still burns today, but most of the station's buildings are now used as a youth hostel

A Tall Tower and a Taller Tale

Another California lighthouse used as a hostel is the one at Pigeon Point about fifty miles south of San Francisco. Built in 1872, the brick tower is imposing. It soars 115 feet above the ground and more than 160 feet above the ocean. A first-order Fresnel lens once shone from the lofty lantern room, but in 1972 it was replaced by an aero-marine beacon.

State park interpretive specialist Nelson Morosini gives tours of the lighthouse and offers guests a solid grounding in the "real" history of navigational lights. "People are in awe of and in love with lighthouses because they take them back to what we all think was a kinder and gentler era," he says. "We see the old lighthouse keeper sitting by the fire with his feet up, reading an Emily Brontë novel, and sipping a glass of port while the light rotates lazily over his head. Well, here at Pigeon Point we tend to explode that myth."

Life at light stations in California and elsewhere was certainly a lot harder and less romantic than people imagine. Visitors to Pigeon Point may learn about what life was really like for keepers and their families. But they may also encounter a myth or a tall tale or two. For instance, there is the story about the unfortunate Sarah Coburn and her missing stomach.

"It's a ghost story," says Morosini. "Sarah Coburn was the wife of Lorne Coburn, who at one time owned this property. He was unanimously disliked by the locals. Lorne probably sued and

The 115-foot tower of the **Pigeon Point Lighthouse** soars over the Pacific. Although it still serves mariners, the station is now part of a popular state park.

As evening approaches, the **Pigeon Point Light** wakes up. Like many lighthouses, this one has its own spine-chilling ghost story.

got sued by everybody in San Mateo County. When he died, he was mourned by no one with the possible exception of his wife, Sarah."

The unfortunate Sarah did not mourn for long. Morosini paints a ghastly picture of her end. "One morning Sarah Coburn was found brutally murdered in her home with blood on the walls and a blood-stained two-by-four beside her. The local constabulary was unable to determine who killed Sarah, but an autopsy was done and her organs were stored at a local physician's office. Before it could be tested, her stomach turned up missing."

The stomach was never seen again, but Sarah herself occasionally puts in an appearance. Or so it is said. "When the fog is in at night here at Pigeon Point and you look up at the tower, it's not unusual to see the image of Sarah Coburn outside the lantern room," says Morosini. "Possibly she is looking for the person who sent her to her death. Or she may just be looking for her lost stomach."

Nelson Morosini

127

Socialites and Seals

A less gruesome sort of ghost haunts the Point Pinos Lighthouse on the fabled and remarkably beautiful Monterey Peninsula. Forming the southern rim of the broad Monterey Bay, the peninsula is noted for its ocean scenery, sea otters, and extraordinary number of seals. The rich and the famous gather here to relax, play golf, and hobnob with movie stars in upscale peninsula communities such as Carmel, Pacific Grove, and Pebble Beach. More modest than the peninsula's multi-million-dollar mansions, but no less impressive, is a Cape Cod–style structure located at the edge of a lush golf course in Pacific Grove. Built by Francis Gibbons in 1855, it is the oldest standing lighthouse on the West Coast.

Bruce Handy

Point Pinos Light

Now a maritime museum as well as an operating lighthouse—its third-order Fresnel lens remains in use—the building is open to the public on weekends. The interior looks much the way it did when Emily Fish, the station's most famous keeper, lived and worked here.

The wife of a prosperous Oakland physician, Fish lived an active social life, rubbing elbows almost daily with California notables. But in 1891 her husband died, leaving her with limited financial resources. Using her extensive personal connections, she secured a job as keeper of the Point Pinos Lighthouse. Here, with the help of her Chinese servant, Que, she carved out a comfortable if not elegant existence and eventually earned a reputation as the "Social-Light Keeper of Point Pinos."

"She entertained extensively," says docent Bruce Handy. "Every Sunday between two and four she hosted a high tea for sea captains, politicians, and famous people."

But Fish did not neglect her duties as keeper. "Lighthouse Service inspectors always gave her an extremely high three-star rating," says Handy.

Apparently the lady lighthouse keeper expected the same commitment from those who worked for her. She was a tough boss. "She fired thirty-two assistants during her time here," says Handy. "She fired them for this or for that but mostly for inefficiency."

Fish lived at Point Pinos until 1914 when she retired at the age of seventy-one. She then moved to a home in Pacific Grove where she lived, and continued to entertain, until 1931. But it was at the Point Pinos Lighthouse where she made her lasting mark and where she can best be remembered. Every room there is filled with her irrepressible spirit.

Flashing out to sea from its sandstone mountain, **Point Sur Light** alerts mariners to the dangers of the rugged–and spectacular–Big Sur coastline stretching more than 100 miles to the south.

Building this lighthouse on the Sur's sheer cliffs presented the Lighthouse Service with one of its greatest challenges.

A Three-Ton Brake Light

I n 1935, only a few years after Emily Fish passed from the scene, another grand lady met her end on the central California coast. She was the 780-foot dirigible *U.S.S. Macon*, one of the largest airships ever to float on air. In one of history's most unusual sea disasters, the helium-filled U.S. Navy dirigible went down in a squall not far off Point Sur, about thirty miles south of the Monterey Peninsula. High winds ripped off part of the airship's tail section, tearing a hole in its helium bags and causing it to lose buoyancy. The *Macon* never recovered and crashed into the ocean with a loss of seventy-three lives.

While the Point Sur Light could do nothing to save the *Macon* or its crew, the beacon has certainly saved countless seamen over the years. The rugged Big Sur coast, where a craggy chain of mountains drops straight down into the ever-churning Pacific, is death to ships. Their only safe choice is to keep well out to sea, and since 1889 the powerful beacon of the Point Sur Lighthouse has warned them to do just that.

Building a light station on Big Sur's nearly vertical cliffs was once thought impossible, but by the late 1880s, with the tally of lost ships and seamen growing with each new storm, the

Lighthouse Service was finally forced to take up the challenge. A special railway had to be built to bring materials to the construction site on Point Sur, a rugged mountain of sandstone. Two years and more than $100,000 were required to complete the granite lighthouse. Once ready for service, it was fitted with a first-order Fresnel lens. The light it focused reached out over the Pacific from an elevation of more than 250 feet and could be seen from up to twenty-five miles away.

When the station was automated in 1972, the Fresnel lens was removed from the tower and hauled away to be placed on display at the Stanton Center in Monterey. Although the big lens is no longer at Point Sur, docent Jaci Pappas nonetheless makes it a highlight of her weekend lighthouse tours. She asks visitors to imagine the huge prismatic lens all but filling the sizable Point Sur lantern room.

"She is a magnificent piece of work," says Pappas, describing the missing Fresnel. "She stands over ten feet tall, she's over six feet in diameter, and she has over a thousand prisms."

Pappas explains that Point Sur's three-ton Fresnel lens worked in a manner not unlike the plastic brake lights on automobiles. "Your tail lights use the same technology," she says. "That's why that tiny little bulb shines so bright when you step on your brakes."

The optic now in use at Point Sur is an aero-beacon similar to those that help pilots find airports at night. "But the light still has the same characteristic," says Pappas. "It flashes once every fifteen seconds. That way if someone is sailing along this coast at night and sees this light, they'll know they are just off Point Sur."

Painted Lifescape

Holly Fassett

With the help of the Point Sur Light, Holly Fassett can always find home. The tower and its beacon, like the mountains and seascape of Big Sur, have provided the scenic backdrop for much of her life.

Fassett's parents were the founders of Nepenthe, the well-known and loved restaurant that looks out over crashing Pacific waves and a seemingly endless stretch of Big Sur scenery. Now she owns the business, and it is a good one. There are few dissatisfied diners in a restaurant where the view through the windows is worth five times the price of anything on the menu.

"My parents had wanted to start out small, to put a hamburger stand down on the highway," says Fassett. "But the local people didn't want that. So my mother said, 'Let's build it in the back where they get the beautiful view.'"

Nepenthe is a Greek word meaning "no sorrow," and it is easy to understand how this place got that name. "That's a pretty good word for it," says Fassett. "You have to meander up a path to get here, and by the time you do, you've left all your worldly cares behind."

Point Sur Light

Fassett says she always loved Big Sur and the view from the restaurant—how could she not? But when she was a child, the lighthouse seemed a chilly and remote place. "When I would get on the school bus, it would go down the coast, and one of its stops was the lighthouse," says Fassett. "It was usually very windy there and often very mysterious. I can remember thinking that I wouldn't want to live there."

Fassett's impressions of the lighthouse have changed over time. For many years she devoted most of her energies to raising her children and helping with the restaurant or running it. Then about five years ago she took up landscape painting. Ironically, the Point Sur Lighthouse is her favorite subject.

"When I was growing up, there were always a lot of artistic people around," she says. "Henry Miller and all kinds of people who were very far out. But not me. I was, like, very, very shy. Someone said I was like the silence after a storm."

Now Fassett puts her silences down on canvas. She sells many of her paintings, and her lighthouse pictures are especially popular. "It's really exciting," she says. "I wish I could go on painting the lighthouse forever."

Guarding a Natural Treasure

The Point Sur Light guards a coast like none other on this planet. Motorists driving the hundred-mile stretch of California Highway 1 from San Simeon to Monterey are often surprised to find themselves climbing higher and higher into the Santa Lucia Mountains. No matter how high they go, the Pacific Ocean is usually just a few yards to the west—and a thousand feet or more below. Brake lights get a lot of use on this road.

Anyone who has ever seen Big Sur would readily agree with conservationist Margaret Owings that it ranks among our nation's foremost

Margaret Owings

natural treasures. But when Owings gazes out over this magnificent land-and-seascape, she sees more than mere scenery. She sees a spiritual challenge and a personal responsibility.

"Big Sur puts people in their place," says Owings, who played a leading role in successful efforts to pull California's sea lions and sea otters back from the brink of extinction. "It puts life in perspective. The mountains roll down to the sea, and the water goes out to infinity. People who come here find that they have to come back because this place has done something to them."

Owings has felt close to the natural world since she was a child. "I was born that way, I think," she says. "Someone gave me Albert Schweitzer to read when I was ten years old, and I said, 'Now here's a man who believes just the way I do.'"

For Owings, Big Sur is home and has been for much of her life. "Each morning when I wake up, swing my feet over the bed, and look down the coast, it comes over me again how grateful I am for the privilege of living here. But I know that with this privilege goes a responsibility to guard not just the wildlife and growing things, but the great immensity of this coast."

Circles and Triangles

About half an hour's drive south of Monterey and some two hours north of San Simeon is the village of Big Sur. All but hidden by groves of soaring redwoods, it is possible to drive right through the place without ever knowing you have been there. In addition to Pfieffer State Park and its coastal sequoias, there are a few rustic motels, campgrounds, and backpacking supply stores, but that is about all.

The Post Ranch, the rather exclusive inn a few miles from the village, is even easier to miss, but that is just the way the owners want it. The unique architecture of the inn's widely spaced guest units causes them to blend in with the cliffs and trees. Most buildings fight with their surroundings, but not these. They appear to be part of the landscape, to have grown up naturally right out of the gravelly soil.

"Circles and triangles," says Myles Williams, attempting to explain the secret of the nearly invisible buildings at Post Ranch. Williams is part owner of the inn. "The architect said we could build round units and triangular units and not have to cut any trees."

A former lead singer for the New Christy Minstrels, the folksy 1960s musical sensation, Williams became a partner in the Post Ranch project several years ago when it became apparent that this historic Big Sur property might fall into the hands of "insensitive developers." Says Williams, "We thought we could build something really environmentally sensitive. So that is what we proceeded to do."

Experienced hotel managers were dubious of the inn's proposed design. Williams recalls

Myles Williams

what they said: "Miles, you can't get furniture into those round and triangular units. And those wedge shapes are so tight you can't even walk into the corners."

As it turned out, the furniture fit perfectly. Apparently, guests at this decidedly upscale hotel are just too overwhelmed by the Big Sur scenery to care much about tight corners. Advertised only by word of mouth, the thirty-unit Post Ranch Inn has been a resounding success.

Hollywood's Favorite Lighthouse

Southern California is famous for movies and the sun, and the sparkling white Point Vicente Lighthouse fits right in here. Located off Palos Verdes Drive near Los Angeles, this handsome light station is a Hollywood favorite. It has been the setting for countless feature film and television scenes.

Like other successful film stars, the Point Vicente Station is always suitably decked out for the part it is expected to play. No makeup or makeover is required. The sixty-seven-foot cylindrical tower rises from a grassy lawn near the edge of a cliff dropping down about a hundred feet to the Pacific. Its cross-hatched windows hint at the exotic while not seeming entirely out-of-this-world. Surrounded by swaying palms, it perfectly suits our most romantic notions of what a southern California lighthouse ought to look like.

Built in 1925, the Point Vicente Lighthouse dates to the early days of southern California movie making. Unlike most

Southern California's **Point Vicente Lighthouse** adds its warm glow to a southern California sunset. Built in 1925, this attractive tower has been featured in many films.

movieland septuagenarians, however, it still has all its original equipment. Its veteran third-order Fresnel lens still shines each night, warning mariners with a powerful flash that can be seen from up to twenty miles at sea.

As one might expect, Point Vicente has its own resident ghost. It is said that on especially foggy nights a lady dressed in flowing robes appears here and there in the vicinity of the tower. Supposedly, she is the former lover of a sailor who died in a shipwreck off Point Vincente. Coast Guard skeptics claim the heartbroken lady is actually an optical illusion generated by minor flaws in the station's lens. On occasion, these can illuminate a stray patch of fog and create a ghostly image.

To get a good look at the lighthouse, if not its fog-shrouded ghost, visitors should stop at the nearby Point Vicente Interpretive Center. The station itself is still an active Coast Guard facility and is closed to the public.

Committee of Two Authors

Not nearly so showy as the Point Vicente Lighthouse is its neighbor just down the coast at Point Fermin. Built during the 1870s, the Point Fermin Lighthouse was not intended as a major coast station, but rather to guide vessels into San Pedro Harbor, the primary sea link for what was then the sleepy town of Los Angeles. For efficiency's sake, the square, four-story tower and keeper's residence were constructed as a single unit, but the structure was nonetheless attractive. A handsome design had been chosen for it: Italianate with touches of decorative Victorian gingerbread.

This comely little lighthouse was one of a matched pair. The same year it was built, its twin was constructed at Point Hueneme about fifty miles up the coast. Both stations were equipped with a fourth-order Fresnel lens and both went into service on the same day: December 15, 1874.

Having served several generations of mariners, the Point Hueneme Light finally fell victim to time, neglect, and rot. The same might have happened to its sister lighthouse at Point Fermin except for the efforts of a determined committee of two.

During World War II, the Point Fermin Light was darkened as part of a general security blackout of the Pacific coast. The lantern was removed so that the tower could be used by spotters watching the horizon for enemy ships and planes. After the war the light was never restored and the old station fell into disrepair. The unsightly watchtower platform was dubbed "the chicken coop," by area residents, but despite the building's rundown appearance, it remained for many a cherished landmark.

One day during the early 1970s, maritime museum director John Olguin received a troubling telephone call. "I'm a civilian employee for the United States Coast Guard," said the caller. "And if you tell anybody that I called, I'll get fired. But I wanted you to know that I just found out they're going to come in and bulldoze the Point Fermin Lighthouse."

"Over my dead body," replied Olguin, who immediately set to work on a letter of protest. Two days later, the letter was published in the Los Angeles newspapers.

One of those who read Olguin's remarks was Bill Olesen, a retired ship's carpenter. The two men were soon in contact and found that they were thoroughly committed to saving the Point Fermin Lighthouse.

"We shook hands, and from then on we had breakfast together once a week at seven o'clock in the morning," says Olguin. "We planned and schemed how we were going save the lighthouse."

Faced with negative publicity, the Coast Guard abandoned its plan to tear down the century-old building. Eventually, it was turned over to the city of Los Angeles for use as the centerpiece of Point Fermin City Park. But without a lantern it still did not look much like a lighthouse.

"I want to take that chicken coop off there and rebuild it the way it was," Olesen said over breakfast one morning.

"So do I," said Olguin. And in time, the necessary funds were raised, and the lantern was restored to its original appearance.

These accomplishments were particularly satisfying for Olesen. "I started going to sea with my father when I was two years old," he says. "I learned the importance of lighthouses for navigators and that my dad's ship came home safely thanks in part to the lights. To me lighthouses like this one at Point Fermin are noble structures designed to serve humankind and guide sailors at sea."

Point Fermin Light

While the lighthouse now looks much as it did in 1874, the station's classical lens has not been returned to its lantern room. Olesen and Olguin hope to see it reinstalled and put back into service.

"I'd like to see that light back at Point Fermin before Bill goes to heaven," says Olguin. "He's ninety-four, he's not going to live to be one hundred and ninety-four, and more than anything else I pray that somehow the good Lord will see to it that light comes back over where it belongs. When it does, folks, we are going to have the biggest party at San Pedro you've ever seen. We are going to dance in the streets. We are going to have bands out here. And we are going to celebrate the fact that this lens came all the way from France, that it served here since 1874, and that it has now been reinstalled where it belongs on top of the Point Fermin Lighthouse."

Dragon Fires

The first mariners who approached the rugged and dangerous California coast had no navigational lights to guide them. The high-masted sailing ships of Spanish explorers who came here during the seventeenth and eighteenth centuries groped along a totally dark and unknown shoreline, often paying with their lives for their adventurous spirit. Later, Spanish treasure ships from the Orient aimed for California as they crossed the five-thousand-mile-wide Pacific. But in all their weeks on the open ocean, they were rarely in such danger as when they once more came within sight of land. There, waiting to ambush them, California's ship-killing rocks lurked all but invisible behind curtains of fog.

It is said that Spanish and Mexican settlers built fires on cliffs and hillsides to guide mariners safely to port. Perhaps these first keepers were merchants anxious to bring their freighters ashore and make a profit. Who knows? But one of the places where the maritime signal fires likely were built was Point Loma near San Diego.

Several years after the United States acquired California from Mexico in 1848,

One of the West's first light stations, the **Old Point Loma Lighthouse** near San Diego dates to 1855. Shining from atop a 400-foot cliff, its beacon was frequently obscured by fog. In 1891 the government commissioned a new Point Loma Lighthouse built at a more practical elevation.

the government chose Point Loma as the logical site for one of the West's first lighthouses. Like many other early California lighthouses, this one was a Cape Cod–style combination tower and dwelling. Although locally quarried sandstone was used in construction, the project cost $30,000, a small fortune at the time. This hefty price appeared even less attractive to lighthouse officials when it was discovered that the forty-foot tower was not built according to specifications. The mistake became all too apparent when the station's first-order Fresnel lens arrived from France and could not be fitted into the skinny lantern room. Since the light was desperately needed, a third-order lens was installed and the original first-order lens shipped far to the north for use at Cape Flattery in what is now Washington State.

Although the tower was relatively short, lofty Point Loma placed the focal plane of the light more than 450 feet above sea level. Even with its less powerful third-order lens, the station threw out a beacon visible from up to forty miles on a clear day. But on most days low-lying clouds and fog banks blanketed the point and made the light invisible to the mariners who needed it most, those approaching the San Diego Harbor.

In 1891, only thirty-six years after they were first lit, the lamps of the Old Point Loma Light were snuffed out. Simultaneously, a seventy-foot, iron-skeleton tower built at a lower, more practical elevation, went into service. The original third-order Fresnel lens brought down from the old Point Loma Lighthouse still focuses its light.

Both these historic lighthouses remain standing. The Old Point Loma Lighthouse up on the cliffs is now a favorite attraction of Cabrillo National Park. Beautifully maintained and furnished in nineteenth-century style, it serves as a memorial to generations of Western light keepers and to the mariners who for hundreds of years have braved the Dragon Coast.

PACIFIC
NORTHWEST

Lights of the

Wilderness Coast

Vancouver •

Lime Kiln Light

Cape Flattery Light

Strait of Juan de Fuca

Victoria

San Juan
Islands

New Dungeness Light

Destruction Island Light

Everett •

West Point Light

Alki Point Light

Seattle •

*Puget
Sound*

Point Robinson Light

Tacoma •

Olympia •

Aberdeen

Grays Harbor Light

North Head Light

Cape Disappointment Light

Columbia River

Astoria

Tillamook Head Light

Yaquina Bay Light

Yaquina Head Light

Newport •

Heceta Head Light

Florence •

Umpqua River Light

Coos Bay •

Gateway to the Wild

America's Pacific Northwest owes much of its bold character and dramatic history to three legendary waterways. One of these is the commercially vital and environmentally sensitive Columbia River, which once served as a long liquid trail for explorers Lewis and Clark and the pioneers who followed them west. Another is the extensive arm and hooked claw of ocean reaching almost all the way around the Olympic Peninsula. Consisting of the Strait of Juan de Fuca, Admiralty Inlet, and Puget Sound, it stretches far inland to connect Seattle, Tacoma, and Olympia with the distant Pacific. The third is a heavily trafficked maritime highway skirting the rugged outer coasts of Oregon and Washington and linking industries to markets all along the Western seaboard. This stormy and rock-strewn north-south route ranks among the nation's most perilous shipping channels.

In fact, all of these waters are dangerous. That is why, nowadays, almost anywhere Northwesterners can smell salt water, they can see the flash of navigational lights. But, of course, that was not always the case. The Pacific Northwest was once a dark and mysterious place, an empty space on the map of the continent.

Even today, much of this expansive region remains wild. Vast stretches of it have changed little since the explorers Meriwether Lewis and William Clark first laid eyes on the Pacific at the mouth of the Columbia River in 1805. Lewis and Clark came here in search of a convenient trade route for American goods and produce. Instead they found what seemed to them a desolate hell of rain-drenched mountains, fog-shrouded cliffs, and fractured rock incessantly pounded by huge waves. Fraught with dangers for shipping, it was a place unlikely to nurture maritime commerce, and that is what they reported to President Thomas Jefferson when they returned to the East the following year.

For centuries this unforgiving coast was seen as bleak and forbidding by mariners who kept well away from its unmarked capes and uncharted inlets. Those who ventured too close more often than not paid dearly. Seamen whose ships foundered here faced near certain death by starvation and exposure or at the hands of hostile native warriors. More than a few Spanish, British, and American vessels driven ashore by raging Pacific storms simply disappeared along with their crews from the historical record, their stories never to be told.

Stephen Beckham

"In 1850 the coast was as it had been for centuries: a rugged wilderness of forests, headlands, and crashing surf," says Stephen Beckham, a history professor at Lewis and Clark College in Portland, Oregon. Beckham specializes in the history of navigational lights. His scholarly interest in them has a personal dimension—both his father and grandfather were lighthouse keepers.

A familiar seamark to lumber freighters, the **Cape Arago Lighthouse** guides ships into Coos Bay. The light is a welcome sight to mariners navigating one of the rockiest and most dangerous stretches of the American coast.

"This was an exposed, uncharted, and dangerous shoreline," says Beckham. "At best only the major headlands or capes were known."

Until the 1850s few efforts were made to mark the Northwest coast and guide mariners clear of its deadly obstacles. Building lighthouses in this remote region was believed far too expensive if not all together impossible. But this attitude quickly changed when gold was discovered at an obscure California mill in 1849. With a flood of Gold Rush prospectors, settlers, and financial investment pouring into the West—mostly by sea—the U.S. government began to look for ways to make the nation's Western coasts safer for ships.

The Eastern and Great Lakes states had long benefited from their own highly effective networks of navigational lights. Now lighthouse officials set to work devising a similar system for the West.

"The plan was to create a series of major coast lights arranged so that any mariner as much as twelve to fourteen miles out would be able to see at least one of them," says Beckham. "The lights were supposed to overlap with Tatoosh Island, Destruction Island, Grays Harbor, North Head, and Cape Disappointment, coming into view one after the other right on down the coast."

Each beacon was to have a different look or unique set of flashes to serve as its signature and help set it apart from all the others. Information on the lights and their distinguishing characteristics would appear in an annual federal publication called the *Coast Pilot*. "Mariners out there in the dark could look toward the shore, see a light, and then look in the *Pilot* and get a clear reading on where they were located," says Beckham.

Construction of the lighthouses that were to make possible this sort of by-the-book navigation began about 1854. After hurriedly completing several towers in California, government crews loaded up their supply ships and headed north. The first lighthouse they built in the Northwest would stand atop the very cliffs where Meriwether Lewis first gazed out at the Pacific.

Graveyard of the Pacific

The mouth of the mighty Columbia was one of the most strategic—and hazardous—points along the nation's entire Pacific coast. This broad portal had served as a gateway for explorers and pioneers, and by the 1850s it had become an important maritime highway as well. The river was the route of choice to Portland and the heart of the inland West, but getting into it from the open ocean was very dangerous. Ships were lost here at an alarming rate.

"The coasts of Oregon and Washington were particularly dangerous in the early decades because that was still the era of sail travel," says Beckham. "When vessels were powered by sails, with no steam to assist, they were vulnerable to winds and currents."

The danger was especially acute at the entrances to bays and rivers. "A schooner captain risked everything by going into an estuary like those at Coos Bay or Yaquina Bay," says Beckham. "At any moment the wind could die down, leaving them adrift and helpless. If fog came in, there was the added threat of crashing into a rock, or reef, or the shoreline itself. There were major problems at almost every estuary."

The most treacherous of all the Northwestern estuaries was the one at the mouth of the mighty Columbia. Hundreds of ships struck bottom and sank while trying to cross the river's shallow bar. As a result, mariners came to know—and fear—the Columbia entrance as the "Graveyard of the Pacific."

Because of the importance of this vital waterway and the numbers of ships being lost here, federal surveyors chose a cliff overlooking the Columbia as the site for one of the first lighthouses in the West. This bold headland was known as Cape Disappointment. It had been named by an early Northwestern fur trader who mistook this landfall for another and, recognizing his mistake, sailed away in disappointment. Now the government would try to help mariners avoid making an even worse—and fatal—mistake here, that of running aground on the bar.

The project got off to an inauspicious start. Ironically, the wooden freighter *Oriole* struck the Columbia bar and sank while attempting to deliver materials for the Cape Disappointment tower. No lives were lost in this disaster, but it delayed construction for months. So, too, did the steady downpours that left the site knee-deep in mud. But the lighthouse was finally completed and its lamps lit on October 15, 1856.

The Cape Disappointment Lighthouse was built to last. Today, it looks much the same as it did on the day it entered service almost a century and a half ago. The fifty-three-foot masonry tower is five feet thick at the base and two and a half feet thick at the top. But even this fortresslike structure has its decorative touches—for instance, eagle-headed gargoyles.

Befitting its significance, the Cape Disappointment Station received the most powerful optic available, a first-order Fresnel lens. The giant prismatic lens served here until the turn of the century when it was transferred to the nearby North Head Lighthouse. Today, a fourth-order lens shines from atop the tower, displaying a red and white flashing light. Like all West Coast beacons, this one is automated, its workings monitored electronically by the Coast Guard Aides to Navigation team in Astoria.

Although this historic lighthouse is not open to the public, visitors to the adjacent Fort Canby State Park are invited to walk the grounds and enjoy the magnificent scenery. A stop at the park's Lewis and Clark Interpretive Center will help put the view into historical perspective.

While the Cape Disappointment Lighthouse, Fort Canby Park, and the nearby North Head Lighthouse are located in Washington State, they are all within easy reach of Portland and Astoria, Oregon. With its many fine, old homes, Astoria itself is a popular tourist attraction. Berthed on the Astoria waterfront is the Lightship *Columbia*, which once helped guide vessels across the river's treacherous bar.

North Head Lighthouse marks the northern approaches to the mouth of the Columbia River, one of the nation's most important waterways. The modern aerobeacon in use here replaced a first-order Fresnel lens, now on display in a nearby museum.

Surfboats to the Rescue

The Cape Disappointment Coast Guard Station remains active, and for the men and women who serve here, a lot of history can be packed into only a few moments. They are guardians of the Columbia River bar. Often called on to rescue pleasure boaters, fishermen, and seamen in distress, they put themselves at risk to save others.

"It's not your mundane, eight-to-five job, that's for sure," says coastguardsman Bart Pope. "I think you have to be a little bit of an adrenaline junkie to do this."

Pope and others at the station pilot the powerboats that challenge the formidable Pacific surf during rescue operations. These remarkable, fifty-foot boats are designed to cut through thirty-foot swells and breakers. They can roll completely over in the waves and pop back to the surface undamaged. The well-trained coastguardsmen have strength, reflexes, and skills to match the durability of their highly maneuverable surfboats. Even so, the Columbia River bar puts both the boats and their pilots to a severe test.

"The Columbia River bar is noted for some of the roughest sea conditions in the world," says Pope. "In one direction you have waves coming in off thousands of miles of unobstructed water. In the other you have a powerful outgoing current, which at times can create significant waves. On a rough day, you can have fifteen- to-twenty-foot breakers in this area."

The formidable surf can tear sizable vessels to pieces in a matter of minutes, but the surfboats bob up and down in the waves like corks. It can be a wild ride. "You may get a breaker coming straight in off your bow, another one that's starting to break off to your side, and another that's breaking off your starboard," says Pope. "It's coming at you from three different directions, and when that happens, the only thing you can do is eat it."

Jeff Streich

Once considered one of the West's most important lighthouses, the 1856 **Cape Disappointment** tower is set atop a rocky headland commanding the entrance to the Columbia River. It now displays a fourth-order, alternating red and white beacon.

Bart Pope

Obviously, the job of a surfboat pilot is a dangerous one. "There have been times when those boats went out, capsized, and lost their crews," says Pope.

Over the years, in the Columbia River area alone, twenty or more surfboaters have died while trying to save the lives of others. Most of those losses were among members of the old Lifesaving Service, disbanded during the 1930s. The small, wooden surfboats and other equipment used by the old-time lifesavers were primitive by comparison to those available to their modern, Coast Guard counterparts. "You're talking about guys who would row open boats across this bar," says Pope. "I can't even imagine that, to tell you the truth."

On the other hand, most of us can't imagine the things Pope does on almost a daily basis. "I don't think anybody does it for the money," he says. "It's not the highest paying job in the world. I think people do it for the satisfaction of helping somebody else in trouble."

Light at North Head

In addition to the Cape Disappointment Lighthouse, the approaches to the Columbia are marked by a second major navigational station. Only about two miles north of the cape is the North Head Lighthouse. Completed in 1898, it has now served mariners for more than a century.

By the 1890s mariners had begun to question the effectiveness of the Cape Disappointment beacon. Frequently obscured by fog and mists rising off the river, this light was often of limited use to seamen, especially those approaching from the north. The cliffs at North Head made it difficult or impossible to see the beacon from the decks of southward bound vessels.

Following a series of disastrous wrecks, lighthouse officials decided to

North Head keeper's house

establish a second station on North Head itself. Once completed, the new station's sixty-five-foot tower was fitted with the first-order lens previously in use at Cape Disappointment. The latter station was then demoted to a lesser status and given a smaller fourth-order lens.

Nowadays, the North Head Lighthouse guides mariners with a modern, airport-style beacon, which can be seen from up to twenty miles at sea. The grand first-order lens that once served here and at Cape Disappointment is now on display at the nearby Lewis and Clark Interpretive Center.

But even without its old first-order classical lens, North Head Light Station is impressive and has much to offer visitors. "It's a complete light station," says Barb Kachel, who con-

Barb Kachel

siders herself an "informal lighthouse keeper." Kachel's husband is a ranger at Fort Canby State Park, and the couple has lived in one of the North Head keeper's residences for about ten years.

Often when the Coast Guard automated light stations, all unnecessary structures were removed. But here at North Head most of the original buildings were left intact. "It not only has the light tower, but also the oil houses, keeper's residences, barn, and chicken shed," says Kachel. "There are two keeper's dwellings, one for the head keeper and another for an assistant."

While the assistant's dwelling is open to tourists as a guest house, the Kachels live in the primary dwelling. "We can see the beacon as it sweeps through the trees from our master bedroom window," she says. "I go to sleep counting the flashes, first one, then twelve seconds later another. That's how I know the light is working. If it is, then I can go to sleep. I've kept an eye on the lighthouse the whole time I've lived here."

Occasionally, Kachel answers questions for tourists. "One thing people ask a lot is, 'Now that I've been to North Head, is it worth it to go on and see Cape Disappointment?'" she says. "They figure that when you've seen one lighthouse, you've seen them all. But that's clearly not the case. These are two very distinct towers."

The two lighthouses and their beacons were made distinct intentionally and for an important reason. It was imperative that mariners be able to tell them apart. Disaster would be the likely result of any confusion. Today, just as in the past, seamen can readily distinguish the fixed white North Head beacon from the red and white alternating light at Cape Disappointment.

Thunderbird Light

Like the Cape Disappointment Lighthouse, the Cape Flattery Light Station on Tatoosh Island in the far northwestern corner of Washington State displays a red and white beacon. But here the colors do not alternate. Instead, the light has a separate "red sector" intended to warn mariners away from ship-killing rocks not far offshore.

Established in 1857, only three years after construction of the Northwest's first lighthouse at Cape Disappointment, the Cape Flattery Light is one of the West's oldest navigational sta-

Photo courtesy U.S. Coast Guard

Besieged by ocean, **Cape Flattery Light**
marks the Strait of Juan de Fuca.

tions. But unlike many other old lighthouses, its beacon remains vital to shipping. Any trouble here or variation in the performance of the light and its crucial red sector will bring a prompt response from the Coast Guard.

Riding a relatively calm and stable column of air, a Coast Guard helicopter descends and settles onto its pad on remote Tatoosh. This desolate place was given its name by the Makah people who once hunted whales off this coast in dugout canoes and who still live on ancestral lands near the cape. It was they who gave Tatoosh Island its name. In the Makah language, Tatoosh is the word for the thunderbird or god of lightning.

Not far from the helicopter landing area, cliffs drop down a hundred feet or more into boiling surf. If the chopper had been a boat and tried to land on this rugged island, the big waves might have smashed it to bits on the rocks. The young coastguardsmen brought by the helicopter are glad of the advanced technologies that have made their trip to Tatoosh a safe one. As members of a Coast Guard Aids to Navigation team, they visit Tatoosh at least four times a year to service the Cape Flattery Lighthouse.

"We come out once every three months to check the light," says Chief Petty Officer J. Franklin, who commands the Coast Guard team. "The electricians go through the battery systems and check the solar panels that supply the power. We make sure everything is working the way it should."

Although most of the equipment at the Cape Flattery station is automated, designed to run by itself, the Coast Guard maintenance work here may take several days. But this visit is special, and it comes late in the year. It is windy and cold on desolate Tatoosh, and, no doubt, the young coastguardsmen hope this stay will be a short one.

LEGENDARY LIGHTHOUSES

Like many of the West's early navigational stations, the 1858 **Cape Flattery Lighthouse** consists of a Cape Cod-style residence with a short tower rising through its roof. The windows at the back of the lantern room have been painted black to prevent unwanted reflections. The station is no longer manned.

Jeff Streich

Until the 1970s, when the light was automated, it could be maintained only by full-time keepers who lived here year-round. Early keepers considered Cape Flattery a hard-duty station. Its extremely remote location made bringing in supplies difficult and cut them off almost completely from civilization. Stiff winds kept the station flag snapping, and storms frequently tore at the stone walls of the dwelling and tower causing them to shake violently. The extreme isolation, terrible weather, and constant fear of attack by Indians resulted in the resignation of the first several keepers who served here.

Fortunately, lighthouse officials were always able to find someone to do the job, for the Cape Flattery Light was an essential beacon. Like the West Quoddy Head Light in the Northeast, Cape Florida Light in the Southeast, and Point Loma Light in the Southwest, it marked one of the strategic corners of the continental United States. It also pointed the way to the Straits of Juan de Fuca, the gateway to Seattle and Canada.

Chief Petty Officer J. Franklin

But the effort to keep the light burning came at a high price. Shut away from all outside contact for months at a stretch, keepers became depressed and easily irritated. Enraged over a minor incident, a keeper in the 1860s fought a duel with one of his assistants. The two men blazed away at one another, but miraculously—or so it seemed—neither was injured. Perhaps thinking themselves among the worst pistol shots in history, the embarrassed lighthouse crewmen were reconciled and, in time, became fast friends. Only much later did they learn that an associate had loaded their pistols with blanks.

On another occasion, a keeper who could no longer endure the loneliness attempted suicide by throwing himself off the cliffs. His assistants found him on the rocks below, broken, bleeding, but still alive. Taken to a hospital on the mainland, he eventually recovered and returned to his duties.

Tatoosh became a little less lonely for its keepers in 1883 when the U.S. Signal Corps built a weather station here. Later a radio compass transmitter was added, and by 1930 the population of keepers, technicians, and family members who lived with them on the island had grown to more than forty. The small but thriving community had its own post office and a schoolhouse where seventeen children attended classes. But in 1966 the weather station closed and its buildings were demolished. Then, in 1977 the lighthouse was automated and the last of the island's inhabitants packed up their belongings and left. Nowadays, the light, fog signal, and other navigational equipment on Tatoosh are monitored from a central Coast Guard facility in Astoria, Oregon.

Although, the Cape Flattery Station is no longer manned, its beacon remains a vital signpost for vessels entering the Strait of Juan de Fuca. Many of the ships that pass by the cape are petrochemical tankers, likely to create an environmental calamity should they run aground or sink along this pristine coast. For these and other reasons, the work Franklin and his team do here during their brief visits is very important.

"People depend on us," states Franklin. "We double-check ourselves several times just to make sure that what we're doing is accurate."

Just now Franklin is concerned about the accuracy of the station's beacon. Recently, the captains of vessels passing by the cape have reported problems with the light. Of particular concern is the beacon's red sector, which covers Ducan Rock and a bank of dangerous shoals just off Cape Flattery.

Franklin's Aids to Navigation team is on Tatoosh Island to find out what is wrong and, whatever that is, fix it. He believes reflections bouncing off the rear windows of the lantern room may be "muddying" the station's signal and confusing mariners. But it is also possible that the red and white sectors are improperly aligned. Tonight the alignment will be checked.

"We're going to have a Coast Guard cutter come through here and use a gyro compass to verify the red sector," says Franklin.

Later, after night falls over Tatoosh Island, a sleek cutter closes in on the cape through the darkness. Over a crackling radio, Franklin monitors its progress. Based on the results of this test, Franklin has several of the windows at the back of the lantern room painted black.

Ironically, blacking out certain windows of a lighthouse can add significantly to the usefulness of the beacon. Navigational professionals understand that precision is as important as the brightness of the light—nowadays, it can be even more important. Just as musicians use carefully timed silences to add emotional power to a melody, Franklin and his team use the dark to fine-tune the beacon of the Cape Flattery Lighthouse.

No Two Alike

Up and down the Pacific coast, navigational beacons each play their own tune. They have each been given distinguishing, signature characteristics that enable mariners to easily tell one light from another. And just as the beacons are distinctive, so too are the towers themselves. Design, paint, elevation, and setting combine to make each one unique. Their histories are unique as well. As is invariably the case with people, each lighthouse is an individual with its own story to tell.

Built in 1891, the Destruction Island Lighthouse, on the remote Pacific coast of the Olympic Peninsula, was long one the least favored lighthouse duty stations. As its name suggests, the island has a dark history. On two separate occasions during the 1700s, foraging parties sent ashore by ships anchored near this island were attacked and slaughtered by Indians.

While the lighthouse keepers here had no trouble with Indians, they were certainly lonely, and life on the island was hard. Much to the relief of the Coast Guard crew, no doubt, the Destruction Island Light was automated in 1989. Although this sentinel now stands watch alone, its beacon still guides mariners with its white flashes spaced ten seconds apart.

Further down the Washington coast is the Grays Harbor Lighthouse. For almost a century it has marked the entrance to a strategic bay shaped like an arrowhead. The pointed far end of the bay presses far inland toward Olympia and falls just thirty-five miles short of linking up with the Puget Sound and making an island of the vast Olympic Peninsula. Rising more than a hundred feet above the dunes, the Grays Harbor tower is the tallest in Washington. The station still has its original third-order Fresnel lens. Its red and white flashes can be seen from up to twenty-three miles away.

One Too Many

Built in 1871, the modest and homey Yaquina Bay Lighthouse was one of Oregon's earliest lighthouses, but oddly enough, it remained in service for only three years. Its light, snuffed out in 1874, was the victim not of storm, erosion, or war, but of a Lighthouse Board decision to build a taller tower on Yaquina Head only a few miles from the existing Yaquina Bay station. Once the impressive Yaquina Head tower was completed, its much smaller neighbor was no longer needed. Even so, the combination tower and dwelling at Yaquina Bay has survived for more than one and a quarter centuries. Today, it is open to the public as a museum offering visitors a fascinating glimpse into the lives of nineteenth-century lighthouse keepers.

Dressed in period costume, museum docent Marie Chinburg greets visitors. "Welcome to the Yaquina Bay Lighthouse, the oldest building in Newport," she says. "I'd like to invite you to come into my parlor."

After its short career as a lighthouse, the structure saw use as a lifesaving station. Then it was boarded up for many years. Now it has been restored and furnished to look as it did

The bright star of the **Yaquina Head** beacon breaks through morning fog and mist. Focused by a classical first-order Fresnel lens, the light can be seen from up to 19 miles away. The station's 93-foot tower is one of the tallest in the West.

during the early 1870s, when a light keeper and his family lived here. "All of the things you will see here might have been in the lighthouse or in any home in the 1870s," says Chinburg.

In step with the growing public fascination with lighthouses, the popularity of the Yaquina Bay Museum has burgeoned. "It's hard to keep them out of here," says Bart Moyer, only partly in jest. Moyer is a member of the Friends of Yaquina Bay, the organization that maintains the lighthouse and operates the museum. "Two or three years ago, visitation was about fifty thousand. Now it's up to around seventy thousand people per year."

Some are afraid the increased traffic may damage the historic lighthouse. "The building is both historic and fragile," says Moyer. "We may have too many people coming through here."

Many who visit the Yaquina Bay Museum also stop at nearby Yaquina Head to see the tower that made the original lighthouse obsolete. Built in 1873, the Yaquina Head Lighthouse remains in operation to this day. Now part of an Oregon state park, its ninety-three-foot tower is the tallest in the state and one of the tallest in the Pacific Northwest. Since it stands on a cliff more than seventy feet above the ocean, its light flashes out toward the Pacific from an elevation of more than 160 feet. The light can be seen from a distance of about nineteen miles.

Visitors to Yaquina Head can enjoy not just the lighthouse, but also the view and the sea life in tidal pools along the shore. "You can see an incredible variety of life just a few feet from the lighthouse," says park biologist and interpreter Ed White. "The keepers would come down here sometimes to get food. The mussels and some of the other sea animals are edible. So the keepers could just take a short walk, come down here, and grab some dinner."

A Menacing Beauty

I t is a long way down to the water at Heceta Head, just north of Florence, Oregon. The light station here is perched on the shoulder of a cliff so sheer and rugged that only the boldest climber would attempt to scale it. The tower itself is only fifty-six feet tall, but because of the considerable elevation of the site, its light shines out toward the Pacific from more than two hundred feet above the waves.

Heceta Head Light

Although taken out of service in 1874, only three years after it was completed, the **Yaquina Bay Lighthouse** still stands. Today it serves as a maritime museum.

Clinging to the face of a precipitous Oregon cliff, the **Heceta Head Light** shines seaward from an elevation of more than 200 feet. Few lighthouses can boast a more beautiful setting.

If the view here doesn't cause drivers along U.S. Highway 101 to hit the brakes, nothing ever will. Heceta Head Lighthouse overlooks a breathtaking expanse of jagged rock, churning surf, and blue ocean—a stunning scene even by the standards of coastal Oregon. But of course, the light station was not built because of the scenery.

The fact is, this is one of the most hazardous stretches of coast in the West. Scores of craggy outcroppings and shoals reach far out into the sea from the mainland, and mariners cannot approach Heceta Head without risking disaster. The Spanish explorer Don Bruno de Heceta took note of the dangers when he charted the area in 1755, leaving his name behind him.

Despite the threat to shipping, Heceta Head was not marked with a light until 1894. Lighthouse officials considered the construction of a tower here too difficult and expensive. When the project was finally undertaken during the 1890s, it proved hugely expensive. The arduous process of shipping materials to the remote headland, hauling them up the cliffs to the site, and building the station a few bricks at a time took more than two years. And it cost the government more than $180,000, a fantastic sum at the time.

The lighthouse proved well worth its hefty price, however. Still solid after a century of use, the tower continues to guide mariners with the powerful beacon focused by its original first-order Fresnel lens. Travelers may be doubly glad of the effort poured into the station by its builders, since they can now enjoy both a good night's sleep and a world-class view by renting rooms in the old keeper's quarters. Mike and Carol Korgan have turned the building into a gracious bed-and-breakfast inn. On most evenings the Korgans lead fascinating walks to the tower, where they can see the station's big lens all lit up like a giant chandelier.

Oysters and Chariot Wheels

The Umpqua River Lighthouse at Winchester Bay, about two hours south of Heceta Head, almost lost its first-order Fresnel to automation. But thanks to protests from local preservationists, the huge lens still throws its powerful light out over the river, bay, and Pacific.

Like the Yaquina Bay, this area is blessed with an abundance of sea life, and no doubt, early keepers supplemented their diet with shellfish. The Umpqua River brings rich nutrients down from the Cascades and dumps them into the bay. Today, jetties near the mouth of the Umpqua help tame the river and also create an ideal environment for aquaculture. Here oysters grow on long strings like rock candy.

"They grow in the water instead of on the bottom, so that there's no taste of bottom sediment," says oysterman Vern Simmons. "They're really clean, they're really white, and they grow twenty-four hours a day."

Simmons's aquaculture operation enables him to harvest boatloads of the delicious mollusks from the Umpqua. "These are two-year-old oysters," he says. "These will go to restaurants in San Diego, Chicago, and Portland, but in the summer tourist season, an awful lot of them just go right out our front door."

The historic Fresnel lens at the Umpqua River Lighthouse, which overlooks Simmons's oystering facility, nearly went out its door some years ago. The machinery that rotates the heavy lens and makes possible its flashing red and white beacon broke down in 1983. Rather than make expensive repairs, the Coast Guard planned to replace the lens with a more easily maintained modern plastic beacon. Faced with unexpected public opposition, the Coast Guard relented and restored the station's old-fashioned chariot-wheel carriage.

The **Umpqua River Lighthouse,** near Winchester Bay, Oregon, still employs its original first-order Fresnel lens. The station and its imported lens date to 1894.

Re-engineering a Fresnel

At the Cape Blanco Lighthouse on the southern Oregon coast, it was the lens, rather than the machinery, that needed recent repairs. Dating to 1870, Cape Blanco is Oregon's oldest operating light station, and it stands guard over some of the West's most threatening waters. Frequently shrouded by fog and battered by storms, the cape has claimed many ships and lives. In 1992 the light station itself suffered damage, but not by way of wind and water. Vandals broke into the tower and, wielding a crowbar, smashed several prisms in the station's fine, old Fresnel lens.

Usually, shattered Fresnels cannot be repaired. In this case, however, Larry Hardin, a talented optician in the nearby town of Bandon, was able to re-create some of the delicate glasswork. Hardin accomplished this seemingly impossible task by using what he calls "reverse engineering," a trial-and-error process that eventually revealed the secret of how the prisms were made.

"I'm romantically attached to glass," says Hardin. "I can't help it. I've been working with glass for, gosh, forty years now, and I still love every minute of it."

But even with all his experience, repairing the Fresnel presented Hardin with a unique challenge. "We weren't able to find a bit of information on how these prisms were originally made," says Hardin. "We had to examine them microscopically to get an idea of the type of machinery that might have been used to make them. Then we had to invent our own equipment that would give us the same shapes and finishes."

Eventually, Hardin was able to replace five of the damaged prisms and a bull's-eye. Now the lens is serviceable again—and just as beautiful as before. Says Hardin, "It's good to know that something built over a hundred years ago is still doing its job and doing it well."

War Canoes, Giant Crabs, and Polished Brass

Like the Cape Blanco Lighthouse far to the south, the historic New Dungeness Light Station on Washington's Strait of Juan de Fuca has benefited from inventiveness. Only here, the innovation is organizational rather technical. A national association of volunteer keepers has returned the station from the dormancy of automation to active life.

The station's earliest keepers might have thought the New Dungeness Spit a poor location for a lighthouse. The spit was a killing ground traditionally used by warriors from villages all along the strait as a convenient place to meet, settle differences, and, occasionally, stain their axes. The often bloody confrontations on the spit continued even after a light-

New Dungeness Light

house was built here in 1857. In fact, the light helped guide the war canoes to their violent rendezvous.

The combatants never molested lighthouse personnel—only one another—but keepers and their families were understandably frightened and horrified. Then, following a particularly ghastly 1868 incident in which eighteen Tsimshian men, women, and children were slaughtered, the intermittent fighting came to an end. An eerie peace settled over the spit, and keepers were able to go about their routine chores without the distraction of flashing tomahawks and the cries of injured combatants.

The work keepers did at the New Dungeness Lighthouse was crucial to Pacific Northwestern shipping and commerce. The beacon guided mariners through the strait and onward to Seattle and other ports on the Puget Sound and in Canada. It also helped them avoid the low, sandy spit, which could barely be seen from the water.

Even with the light there to warn them, ships continued to founder on the spit. In 1868, only weeks after the Tsimshian massacre, the fog-blinded freighter *Atlanta* ran

aground within a few dozen yards of the station. She struck bottom so close to the lighthouse that the captain of the stranded vessel could hear the keeper's family carrying on a conversation over dinner. Luckily, the *Atlanta* suffered little damage and, at high tide, was able to back off the spit and continue on its voyage.

Although now automated, the New Dungeness Light remains an important marker. Even small fishing craft use the light to advantage. One mariner who often follows the beacon's guidance is crabber Jack Collins.

"Well, it looks like we eat tonight," says Crabber Jack, pulling aboard a trap containing several large crabs. The crustaceans he lifts out of the trap are so big that one of them might feed a whole family.

Collins has been crabbing in these waters for more than forty years. The giant crabs he goes after share their

Crabber Jack Collins

name with the nearby spit and its lighthouse. They are called Dungeness crabs and are highly prized for their succulent meat. "They're probably the finest eating seafood around," says Collins. "They're a lot more tasty and a lot sweeter than the king crab or the snow crab."

Crabbing earns Collins a modest living, but like most commercial fishermen, he works hard and puts in long hours. "Years ago I lost my brains, I guess," says Collins. "You have to be half crazy to be a fisherman, but it sure beats working for a living. At least you get to go for a boat ride every day."

The New Dungeness Light plays an important role in Collins's daily routine. The tower helps orient him to the shore and the horizon. In the evening, when he is headed for home, its beacon serves as a convenient guidepost. And if he has an emergency, he can likely get help at the New Dungeness Station, for unlike most lighthouse nowadays, this one is usually occupied.

"There are lots of people like me running around in small boats," says Collins. "Even with all the modern navigation equipment we have today, we really need the lighthouse. If you get into trouble, you can go ahead and beach your boat and know that somebody is going to be there."

With its automated beacon, the lighthouse has no official full-time Coast Guard keeper. However, the New Dungeness Chapter of the U.S. Lighthouse Society licensed the property from the government in 1994 and since that time has maintained a staff of volunteer keepers at the station.

Eric Henriksson

"We took the boarding down from the windows and made it look alive again," says Eric Henriksson, one of the group's founders. "A lot of us have a passion for history. This gave us both a challenge and an opportunity to do something to preserve the past."

The chapter has no trouble finding volunteers willing to pay for the privilege of living and working at the lighthouse. Only society members may serve as keepers, but membership is open to all. Usually, prospective keepers must sign up months in advance to take their turn at New Dungeness.

Mara Mowery

"People are delighted to pay the modest sum we charge them to stay out here," says Mara Mowery, the chapter president. "Some are looking for a week of solitude. Others really get a kick out of guiding visitors around the place. And there are those who love to work at fixing things up. People are into lighthouses every which way."

Serving as a New Dungeness keeper is no vacation. Keepers are expected to work and help maintain the property, but nobody seems to mind. "People want to leave their mark here," says Mowery. "They want to say, 'Well gee, I painted the fence,' or 'I painted the steps,' or 'I did this, that, or the other.' I guess it's more fun to keep up somebody else's house than your own." The most recent keepers polished all the station's brass fittings, a job that took several days.

The Street Lamps of Puget Sound

From Cape Flattery and the open Pacific, the Strait of Juan de Fuca reaches eastward for more than a hundred miles, finally terminating in a maze of passages and inlets known collectively as Puget Sound. Today, thousands of yachts and smaller pleasure craft share the protected waters of the sound with ferries, petrochemical tankers, container transports, and U.S. Navy warships. Navigating these crowded waters can be tricky, but the Puget Sound is well marked.

Over the years more than a dozen lighthouses were built to guide vessels through the narrow, winding channels here. Many are still working aides to navigation. But even those that no longer serve mariners remain objects of intense fascination for historians, artists, tourists, and romantics of every sort.

Among the many fans of the region's historic light stations are Ted and Sharlene Nelson. The authors of two books on lighthouses, the Nelsons have been sailing the Puget Sound for years. Much of their research comes from first hand experience.

"We always try to keep a lighthouse in view as we sail," says Ted Nelson. "We don't have radar, and it's nice to see a light when we come out of the fog."

Unlike beacons on the outer coast, designed to be seen from many miles at sea, the lighthouses of Puget Sound were intended to guide ships through a labyrinth of islands, points, inlets, and channels. "They generally have low towers and small lenses," says Nelson. "Their lights are visible from only twelve to fifteen miles away, but they are always there. They are like street lamps along the road."

Ted and Sharlene Nelson

The sound's intricate system of navigational lights was designed so that mariners nearly always had a beacon in view. "They're placed on prominent points about fifteen or twenty miles apart," says Nelson. "So as you work up or down the sound you can always see a lighthouse. For example, ships sailing out of Tacoma would clear Browns Point Lighthouse as they left Commencement Bay. Then they would have the Point Robinson Lighthouse in view. After Point Robinson, the Alki Point Light would come into view. If they were continuing north, they'd pick up West Point, Point No Point, Maristone, and then Point Wilson."

And so on, one street lamp after another.

Star of the Show

Located on Maury Island just across from Washington's populous Tacoma-to-Seattle metropolitan strip is the small but scenic Point Robinson Lighthouse. It is a popular weekend destination for curious urbanites and tour groups. Visitors are shown around the station by volunteer guides such as Norm Nyhuis and John Thoma, both members of the Coast Guard Auxiliary Flotilla 32.

"The Auxiliary is the civilian component of the Coast Guard," says Nyhuis. "We've taken over a lot of the duties that the Coast Guard can no longer handle because of budget cuts. We do this strictly on a volunteer basis."

The **Point Robinson Lighthouse** on Maury Island in Washington State guides vessels through a heavily traveled stretch of the Puget Sound.

The guides take delight in sharing the history of the station with visitors. "It was originally built in 1885 as a fog-signal station, not a lighthouse," Thoma tells one group. "Then two years later they put a red light on top of a twenty-five-foot open scaffold."

The makeshift station was completely rebuilt in 1915 and given the piece of equipment that marked it once and for all as a true lighthouse: a Fresnel lens. Thoma and Nyhuis consider the station's rather modest fifth-order Fresnel to be the star of their show.

"It's quite frankly irreplaceable and absolutely priceless," says Nyhuis. "It should be protected in a museum some place, but it kind of warms my heart to know that the old girl is still on duty doing what she was intended to do and providing safe passage for mariners."

Long Boat

The first European mariners who came to the Puget Sound had no lights to guide them. During the late 1700s, the British survey ship *Chatham* penetrated the sound as far as Bainbridge Island, across from modern-day Seattle. The captain dared take his square-rigger no farther into these unknown waters and, instead, sent a pair of shallow-draft long boats to explore the uncharted passages to the south. In command of the boats and their oarsmen was one Peter Puget, who in just seven days traveled all the way to the future site of Olympia, now the capital of the state of Washington. Puget took back to the *Chatham* a wealth of information on estuaries, inlets, bays, and navigable channels. He left behind little but his name.

Today, the Vashon-Maury Island Maritime Heritage Society is celebrating Puget's feat by launching a gig, or long boat, similar to those used by early British explorers. Members of the society sing the sea shanty "Haul Away Joe" as they pull their oars in unison and take the boat out on the water.

"Sailors sang shanties when doing work that had to be done together in a certain rhythm," says John Burke, a maritime historian. Burke adds his own booming voice to the chorus.

John Burke

The boat's coxswain interrupts the song. "Port, hold water," he says. "Starboard, prepare to give way." The vessel responds to these commands with a graceful turn. Then it glides onward over the surface of the calm, blue sound.

"This is a ship's long boat," says Burke. "A ship's tender. The explorers took vessels like this into the narrows. That way, if they bumped into anything, they hadn't done much damage to themselves."

With events like the one today, the society teaches traditional boat handling as well as maritime history. Participants get a feeling for the strength and nautical skill required of eighteenth-century seamen. It is far more difficult, however, to convey a realistic sense of the dangers mariners once faced in the confined waters of Puget Sound.

"People think you're safer when close to the land," says Burke, "but nobody ever hits anything out in the middle of the ocean. You hit things when you get close to land. If the *Chatham* had gone aground here, it would have been lost, and the nearest help would have been six thousand miles away."

With its confusion of often fog-shrouded points, the Puget Sound is still a hazardous place for ships. Nowadays, however, mariners can rely on an array of sophisticated navigational aids including radar and satellite-assisted direction finders. But when they need a visual reference or on those rare occasions when shipboard electronics fail them, seamen need only look to the horizon to catch sight of a guiding beacon.

Among the most important of the sound's lighthouses are those marking the entrance to Elliot Bay and the port of Seattle. On the north side of the entrance is the West Point Lighthouse, built in 1881 and still in service today. Its fourth-order Fresnel lens displays an alternating red and white light visible from up to nineteen miles away. Located in Seattle's Discovery Park, the lighthouse is a popular destination for daytrippers and picnickers.

Ships headed north from Tacoma reach Seattle by rounding Alki Point on the south side of the bay. The first humble light on Alki Point was a kerosene lantern hung high on the side of a barn. Later, as commerce between the two cities increased, an official light was established here. The structure seen today dates to 1913 and looks very much like the Point Robinson Lighthouse built at about the same time. Part of an active Coast Guard facility, the station is not regularly open to the public but does occasionally welcome visitors. A guest book in the main building contains the following extraordinary entry, dated September 1, 1954: "Looked on by ye landlubbers with but a passing glance, looked on by ye seafarers as a beacon of hope, ye light must not fail."

So far, the "street lamps" of Puget Sound have not failed.

The diminutive wooden tower of the **Mukilteo Lighthouse** watches over Possession Sound and the Whitbey Island Ferry.

Playground for People and Whales

To the north of Puget Sound and just on the U.S. side of the Canadian border are the San Juans, a chain of 172 unspoiled islands. Although many are little more than scraps of exposed rock, several of the islands are big enough for a scatter of villages and small harbors. Friday Harbor, the largest town in the San Juans, has a year-round population of less than 1,500. Not surprisingly, the pace of life in these islands is slower than on the mainland, and that makes them doubly attractive to city-weary travelers. During the summer months, inbound ferries are crowded with tourists coming to enjoy the natural beauty, fresh air, and relaxed living.

Interestingly, the San Juans are popular not just with people, but also with whales. Often the big marine mammals can be seen playing and feeding just off shore. Boaters plying the sparkling waters surrounding the islands know to keep an eye out for whale spouts.

Lime Kiln Light

Several key navigational lights guide vessels around the outer rim of the San Juans and through the narrow passages between islands. One of these shines from the Lime Kiln Lighthouse on the western side of San Juan, the largest island in the chain. Built in 1914, it was among the last major lights established in Washington State. The station still guides mariners today, but now it has another important function as well. The waterside building serves as home of the Whale Research Center.

"This is an ideal place to study whales," says Rich Osborn, director of the publicly and privately financed Whale Research Program. "Currents

Rich Osborn

coming in from the ocean through the Strait of Juan de Fuca tend to bring in fish, birds, and marine mammals. From May through June whales come by here just about every day, sometimes three or four times a day."

The species seen most often here are the orcas. Popularly known as "killer whales," they feed on seals and large fish such as salmon. The San Juans provide the orcas with an abundance of prey. "The orcas are resident here," says Osborn. "They stay within about two hundred miles of this lighthouse all year around."

The center is studying the clicks, whistles, and other sounds that may very well comprise a whale language. "The lighthouse is close to the shoreline, so we can set up underwater microphones and listen in as the whales pass by. You can recognize the calls of individuals and of groups—they're known as pods. What we want is to sort out the various conversations."

One cannot help wondering what the whales say to one another. What questions do they ask? What answers do they give? As mammals, they share many of our basic experiences of birth, growth, mating, maturity, and death. But in most other ways their lives must be vastly different from our own. For them the Pacific Northwest is still a frontier, a wilderness where the line between life and death, beauty and tragedy is invisibly thin.

Call of the Wild

Located more than a mile off Oregon's northwestern coast, Tillamook Rock lies firmly in the grip of the Pacific. In a storm, mountainous waves sweep over the rock and crash into the walls of the lighthouse that has stood here since 1881. One of the most exposed and isolated navigational stations in the country—if not the world—Tillamook Rock Lighthouse was not well loved by most of the keepers who lived and worked here over the years. Nicknamed "Terrible Tilly" by crewmen, who often fervently wished they were elsewhere, it was a cold, wet, and lonely place. Very few ever asked to be assigned to such remote stations, but one who did was a young coastguardsman named Jim Gibbs.

"I didn't get along very well with the gold braid in the service," says Gibbs. "That's no secret. And so I put in for the most isolated duty I could find."

That turned out to be a job as an assistant keeper at the Tillamook Rock Light Station. According to a traditional adage, to have a wish fulfilled is often the worst thing that can happen to a person. That may very well be what Gibbs thought when he arrived at the Rock.

"I was a relatively young man and the other keepers were much older," he explains. "The only place you could walk was around the perimeter of the lighthouse. At first I thought Tillamook was the worst place in the world."

Jim Gibbs

The Cleft of the Rocks Lighthouse

This early-twentieth-century photograph shows **Tillamook Rock** and its lighthouse under siege by the Pacific. Supplies are being brought ashore by cable from a tender anchored nearby. The Coast Guard abandoned the station in 1957.

But his first sour impression did not last. "The longer I stayed out there, communing with God and nature, the better I got to like it."

When Gibbs was finally reassigned, he was sorry to leave the rock. "It was a vital experience in my life, something I came to really enjoy."

Others did not share Gibbs's appreciation for the rock and were glad when the station was finally closed. Only a few years after Gibbs left Tillamook Rock, its very last keeper locked up the lighthouse and headed for the mainland. The Coast Guard abandoned the station altogether in 1957, but the old building still stands. Recently, it has been put to use in a remarkable but seemingly appropriate way. A Portland-based enterprise called Eternity by the Sea has made the rock a final resting place for human ashes.

As for Gibbs, his years on Tillamook Rock made a lasting impression. Eventually he would become a writer with a special interest in lighthouses and maritime history. Over the years he has authored nineteen books on navigational lights, ships, and the sea.

Today, Gibbs owns a lighthouse, one he designed and built himself. Known as the Cleft of the Rock, it is located near Cape Perpetua, a swirling mass of volcanic rock thrusting into the Pacific near Yahats, Oregon.

"I guess it kind of got into my blood," says Gibbs. "When I was out on Tillamook, I used to say that someday I'd like to have my own lighthouse."

Now he does. Cleft of the Rocks Lighthouse looks out over the Pacific and down onto the Cape Perpetua lava flows. "I thought this would be a very logical place to have a lighthouse," says Gibbs.

The rocks below the lighthouse have a liquid appearance. It is hard to tell where they end and the ocean wilderness begins.

Thunder Bay •

Passage Island Light

Isle Royale

Rock of Ages Light

Rock Harbor Light

Grand Marais Light

Isle Royale Light
(Menagerie Island)

Split Rock Light

Apostle Islands

Devils Island Light

Keweenah
Peninsula

Outer Island Light

Sand Island Light

Michigan Island Light

Duluth •

Bayfield •

Raspberry Island Light

*Lake
Superior*

Whitefish Point Light

Sault S

Marquette •

St. Helena
Island Light

Round

Mackinaw City •

Grand Traverse
Light

Green Bay •

*Lake
Michigan*

Milwaukee •

Grosse Point Light

Chicago •

Chicaogo Harbor Light

Gary •

WESTERN GREAT LAKES

North Channel

Manitoulin Island

Georgian Bay

Bruce Peninsula

Lake Huron

Lights on the Big Lakes

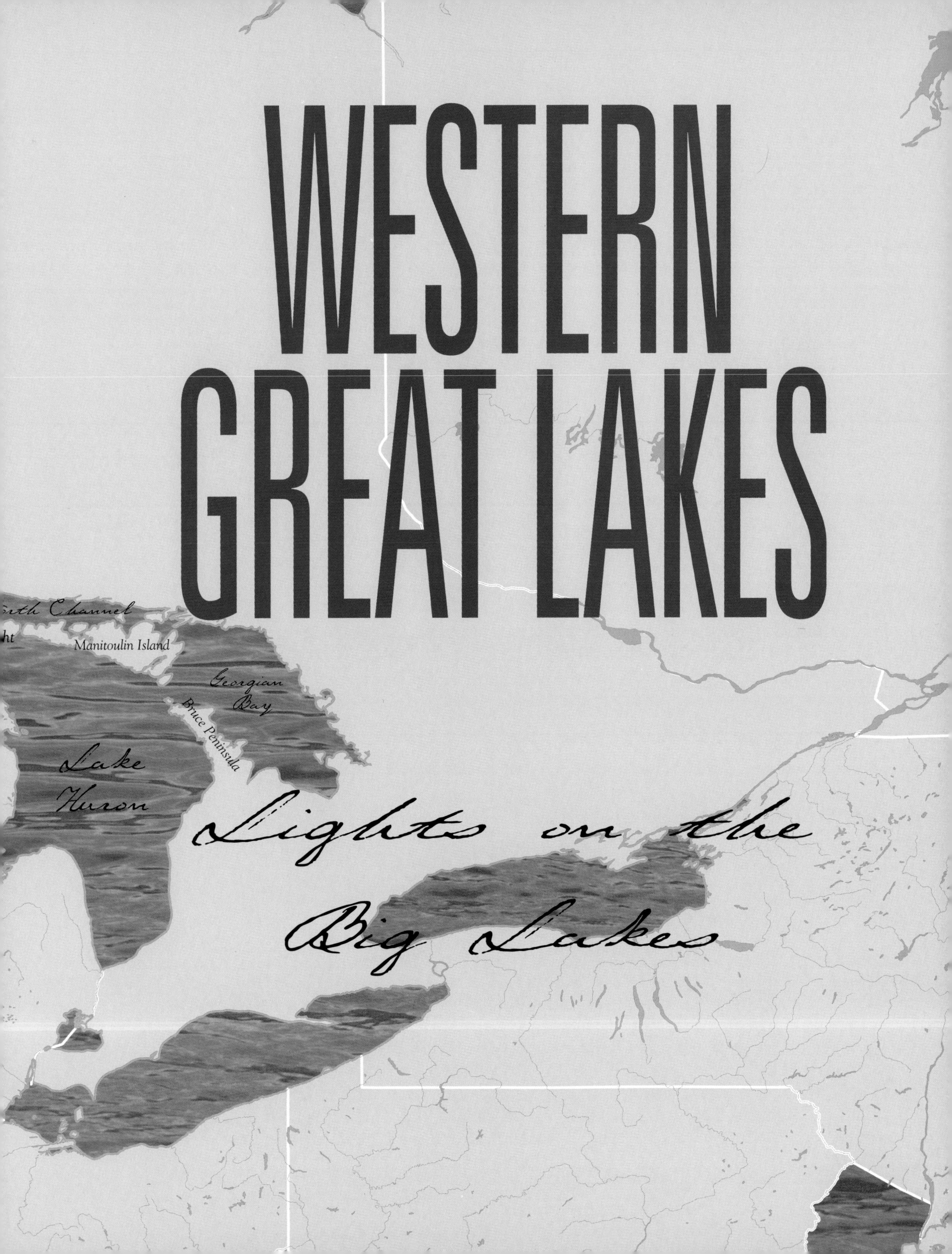

Cleft in the Rock

A Coast Guard service vessel cuts through the slightly choppy waters of Lake Superior. Up ahead a stark white cylinder rises from a seemingly endless plain of blue. This is the Rock of Ages Lighthouse, one of the most remote and isolated navigational stations in the world.

Built in 1908 to mark a ship-killing, open-water shoal, the 130-foot tower was once home to a keeper and three assistants, but not anymore. Since 1978 the station has been automated. Its powerful light and fog signal can do their jobs without the help or watchfulness of human beings. Even so, Coast Guard personnel must make periodic visits to check the equipment.

Today's crossing from the mainland was an easy one. Just now the lake is well behaved, but of course, that is not always so. As experienced freshwater sailors know only too well, it is highly temperamental and its surface is frequently torn by raging storms. The worst may pack hurricane-force winds and throw up fifty-foot swells capable of breaking a ship in half. The lake may be locked in blinding fog for days at a time. Or the skies can be clear, blue, and sunny as they are now.

The good weather is even more welcome than usual as the Coast Guard service crew has brought along a special guest. He is John Tregembo, who served here as an assistant keeper fifty years ago. Then he was an eighteen-year-old coastguardsman. Now, he is retired and has returned with a PBS film crew to pay his old home and workplace a visit.

"Yep. Back at Rock o' Ages," says Tregembo as he steps onto the concrete landing platform. "Fifty years and I'm back here again. Rock o' Ages cleft for me."

Rock of Ages Light Station stands on an utterly barren outcropping of basaltic stone rising a few feet above the water. The lighthouse, only about thirty feet in diameter at its base, is protected from high waves by a massive concrete and steel caisson. Inside the steel-plated tower, a spiral staircase provides access to a galley, a dining area, workshops, storage rooms, and a few small bunkrooms, all stacked one atop the other.

When Tregembo was assigned to the Rock of Ages during the 1940s, his life here was no romantic adventure, but rather a job with long hours and plenty of hard work. He shared the station's confining quarters with a head keeper and two other assistants. Crew members stayed at the station three weeks at a stretch and then received a week of shore leave. While one was away on the mainland, the other three worked rotating shifts, keeping watch over the Rock around the clock.

"You had twenty-one days here and then seven days to go where you wished," says Tregembo. "Of course, with the transportation they had then, you didn't get very far."

John Tregembo, at right

The **Rock of Ages Lighthouse** sits on a massive platform a few miles from Isle Royale in Lake Superior. Until the light was automated in 1978, crew members lived inside the 30-foot-wide tower for six week or more at a time. Usually three crewmen were on duty while a forth took shore leave.

Although the Rock of Ages station was once Tregembo's home, he is now a guest. A young coastguardsman, perhaps not much older than Tregembo was when he lived here, walks through the building with him. Stripped of their furnishings, the rooms are empty, but Tregembo recalls how they looked half a century ago.

"You had two clocks here," he says, spreading his hands at a bare wall. "Seth Thomas, and they had to be right on time. Over there was the radio."

Upstairs on the next level, he points to places where the station's stove and refrigerator once stood. "Sink over here, cabinets over there," he says. "This was the mess deck."

The lighthouse Tregembo remembers no longer exists. The station's interior has suffered from twenty years of neglect, and its living quarters have gone to ruin. But the biggest change is in the lantern room at the top of the tower more than twelve stories above the lake. The imported second-order Fresnel lens that once filled this large round room with glass is gone. The most powerful lighthouse lens ever to shine over the Great Lakes, it was the pride of the Rock of Ages Station. But in 1985 it was replaced by a much smaller, though no less capable, plastic lens.

"The world of plastic," says Tregembo, shaking his head. "Just that one little piece of plastic replaced that beautiful second-order lens."

Later, as he steps back into the Coast Guard boat, Tregembo bids his former home farewell. "See you in another fifty years," he says. "I know you'll be standing. I don't know if I'll be standing though."

Lakes with an Attitude

Those unfamiliar with the inland seas of the American Midwest may be surprised to learn of a lighthouse the likes of Rock of Ages standing in the middle of a lake. But the word *lake* may be something of a misnomer when applied to the *Great Lakes*. These are no ordinary bodies of freshwater.

The lakes are enormous. More than 350 miles long and fully 160 miles wide, Lake Superior covers 31,200 square miles of the continental heartland in a blanket of cold blue water. Some 300 miles long and more than 100 miles wide, Lake Michigan spreads over 22,000 square miles. When Huron, Ontario, and Erie are added to the list, the five lakes have a combined length of more than 1,200 miles. On the east the lakes open to the Atlantic via the St. Lawrence River, and on the west they reach right to the geographic and commercial core of America. Together they impound almost 5,500 cubic miles of freshwater, about twenty percent of our planet's entire surface supply. To get an idea of what that means, consider the following: If the lakes were empty and the Mississippi River could be diverted into them, it would take the Big Muddy more than fifty years to fill them up again.

The tonnage of shipping carried on the lakes exceeds that of the U.S. Atlantic and Pacific coastal waterways combined. Each year thousands of freighters pass through the locks at Sault Ste. Marie, linking Superior with the other lakes, and the Welland Canal,

providing access to the St. Lawrence and the Atlantic Ocean. They carry wheat, corn, coal, iron ore, parts for vehicles, and manufactured goods of every type. In an average season a lake freighter may transport half a million tons of wheat, enough to bake several loaves of bread for every person in the United States. It takes thousands of acres to grow that much wheat and twenty-five long railroad trains to haul it overland to port. In a year's time, a Great Lakes ore freighter may carry enough iron from Duluth to the furnaces in the lower Midwest to make steel for many thousands of cars and trucks. So it is easy to understand why the lakes have been vital to the economic development of the Midwest and the United States as a whole.

Naturally, with all those ships coming and going, the Great Lakes are marked with lighthouses—more than on either of the Nation's seacoasts. Michigan alone has over 130 lights, more than any coastal state. A sparkling, thousand-mile-long chain of beacons stretches from Tibbets Point on the eastern end of Lake Ontario to Duluth at the far western tip of Lake Superior. In fact, there are so many lighthouses scattered across such an expanse of the Midwest that this chapter will limit its focus to Lake Superior, Lake Michigan, and the Straits of Mackinac.

Once, navigation on the Great Lakes would have been next to impossible without lighthouses to serve as traffic signals. The lake shores are relatively low and featureless and

The **North Pier Lighthouse** at the western tip of Lake Superior guides vessels out of Duluth's harbor and into the world's largest body of fresh water. Pier lighthouses like this one are a common sight in the Great Lakes.

their waters chock-a-block with shallows and other threatening obstacles such as John Tregembo's Rock. The lake bottoms are littered with the rotten and rusting hulks of ships that came too close to land or whose masters failed to note the position of a shoal.

However, the greatest dangers faced by sailors on the lakes are the dreaded gales that whip out of the northwest in autumn, often with stunning violence. Usually, they strike in November. It was one such wicked storm in November of 1958 that sunk the 640-foot *Carl D. Bradley*, drowning thirty-five sailors, and another in November of 1975 that took down the famed *Edmund Fitzgerald* along with twenty-nine crewmen.

Among the victims of the Midwest's autumn storms was the very first ship that ever set sail on the Great Lakes. While trekking through the midwest in 1679, the French explorer La Salle built the *Griffin*, a fifty-ton sailing ship, which he hoped would make him rich. Loading it down with beaver pelts, La Salle dispatched the *Griffin* and several of his most trusted men to the East, where he was certain the cargo would sell for a huge profit. Snows had already begun to fall when the *Griffin* pushed off into Lake Michigan. Neither the little ship nor its crew was ever heard from again. Over the centuries since, the lakes have claimed thousands of other vessels and countless thousands of lives.

Many were lost in a single deadly storm in 1913. That year three enormous weather systems swooped down on the Midwest all at once. One poured over the Rockies carrying an immense load of water from the far off South Pacific while another came spinning up from the Caribbean with gale-force winds and a third rushed in from the Bearing Sea with arctic temperatures. The three collided over the Great Lakes on or about November 7, producing what has been described as an inland hurricane.

There had been little or no warning of the storm, and it caught dozens of freighters and passenger liners in open water, far from safe anchorage. High waves battered hulls, and freezing spray coated decks and wheelhouses in a thick layer of ice. Swirling snow squalls blinded captains, pilots, and navigators, while high winds drove their vessels relentlessly toward murderous shoals. The storm raged without pause for five long days. By the time the clouds broke and the winds died down on November 12, more than forty ships had been lost, their hulls shattered by waves or torn apart on rocks. Down with these vessels went 235 passengers and crew. Only a few bodies were ever recovered. Perhaps it is a coincidence worth noting that this calamity took place only a year after the most widely known of all maritime disasters, the sinking of the *Titanic*.

A Night to Remember

Lee Radzak

Every November 10, Lee Radzak pays tribute to the many sailors who have lost their lives on the Great Lakes. He does this in a particularly appropriate way—by lighting up a navigational beacon. Radzak is manager and, in effect, keeper of the Split Rock Lighthouse, now part of a Minnesota state park.

The lighthouse is officially out of service and has been for almost thirty years, but it is still a very busy place. Nearly a hundred thousand people come here each year, making Split Rock one of the most visited lighthouses in the country. A spacious museum not far from the tower retraces the history of the station and of lighthouses in general.

One display describes construction of the lighthouse during the early twentieth century, a feat accomplished with considerable difficulty. Materials had to be brought by small

Waves dash the craggy shoreline below **Split Rock Lighthouse** in the western reaches of Lake Superior. Although it no longer serves as an active aid to navigation, the station is a magnet to tourists attracted in part by the natural beauty of the setting.

boats from Duluth, about fifty miles away, and then hoisted to the top of the 120-foot Split Rock cliffs. The laborers who worked here earned only about thirty-five cents an hour, but their handiwork has stood the test of time. The tower, residences, and a half dozen other structures they built, at a total cost of $72,000, remain solid after almost ninety years.

When the tower was completed during the summer of 1910, it was crowned with a third-order Fresnel lens. Like other Fresnels, this one was imported from France. It is a bivalve-type lens, so-called because it resembles a giant, glass clamshell. A more common type of Fresnel is the beehive or circular-type lens frequently seen in light stations along the Atlantic and Pacific coasts. The clamshell shape of the lens at Split Rock helps it gather and focus more light and makes it unusually powerful. When fully operational, it produced a concentrated beam seen from twenty-two miles out on the lake.

"The lens is the star of the show," says Radzak, who takes obvious pride in its highly polished glass and brass panels. "There are 252 different lens panels, counting both sides. It's massive—about four and a half tons including the revolving apparatus."

The clockwork machinery that turned the lens and caused the light to flash is one of only a few still in working order. According to Radzak, it worked something like an enormous "grandfather or cuckoo clock." The turntable and gears were driven by a cable attached to a 250-pound weight that slowly dropped down through the center of the tower. Every few hours, the mechanism had to be rewound using a hand winch that lifted the weights back to the top of the tower. Keepers assigned to this station had to stay awake throughout the night so they could perform this and other duties.

No one at Split Rock is expected to stay up all night nowadays. By the 1960s the increased use of shipboard radar and radio beacons made the station obsolete, and in 1969 the Coast Guard shut it down. A primary attraction of the park here, the big clamshell lens remains in place, but on most evenings its lamps are dark. Every few weeks the lens is lit as a treat for visiting students or tour groups, but the lighting on November 10 is special. On that night Radzak fires up the beacon in memory of the sailors who lost their lives on that date in the Great Lakes' most famous shipwreck.

Witch of November

The famed wreck memorialized each November at Ship Rock took place just short of three hundred years after the disappearance of the *Griffin*. It happened in the 1970s, an era not of sailing ships, beaver skins, and explorers, but rather—of rock and roll.

Nearly everyone in America has heard Gordon Lightfoot's immensely popular *Ballad of the Edmund Fitzgerald*. It sounds a bit like one of those chanteys sailing men used to sing as they hauled on the lines of a schooner and, as with so many traditional songs of the sea, tells of a ship and crew in trouble. But this is not some seaman's yarn about a seventeenth-century man-o-war sunk by a hurricane down on the Spanish Main, not some *Flying Dutchman* fantasy. It is a true story. The *Edmund Fitzgerald* was a real ship, a modern freighter almost two city blocks long, and one stormy November evening in 1975, the *Fitzgerald* and her crew of 29 vanished—not from the ocean, but from the middle of a lake.

Launched in 1958, the 729-foot Great Lakes freighter *Edmund Fitzgerald* was at that time the world's largest freshwater ship. Known affectionately to her crew as the *"Big Fitz,"* she displaced almost 14,000 tons of lake water and could carry a train-sized, 26,000-ton cargo of reddish iron taconite. During her seventeen years of service, she shuttled back and forth hundreds of times between the loading docks of upper Michigan or Minnesota and the Bessemer furnaces of the lower Midwest, delivering enough ore to make steel for millions of cars. When the *Fitz* left Duluth on November 9, 1975, and headed out into Lake Superior with yet another load of taconite, she was considered to be still in her prime. Her career, however, was about to be cut tragically short.

Around midday on November 10, a mighty gale swept across the lake and began to batter the *Fitz* with thirty-foot waves and seventy-mile-per-hour winds. The storm howled all afternoon and by early evening had done notable damage to the ship. The wind and waves had snapped deck cables, smashed ventilation covers, and wrenched open critical hatches. What was worse, there were signs the ship had started taking on water. She had begun to show a list. But the *Fitz* was in the highly competent hands of Captain Ernest McSorley, who, like his ship, was a veteran of hundreds of voyages on the Great Lakes. He had weathered storms like this one in the past and was confident he could shepherd his big freighter through the mountainous waves and into safe water at the south end of the lake.

As a precaution, Captain McSorley put out a call to the masters of nearby vessels asking them to keep a close watch on the *Fitz*. Only a few miles to the north, the freighter *Anderson* was fighting her way through the same storm. The officers on the *Anderson* had their hands full with problems of their own, but knowing that McSorley's ship had been damaged, they kept an eye on the radar screen, where the *Fitz* showed up as a big green blip. Eerily, when the waves mounted up high enough to block the radar signal, the blip would flicker and disappear. Then, as the *Fitz* climbed up the side of the next huge wave, she would reappear on the screen.

Shortly before 7:00 P.M., an officer on the *Anderson* radioed the *Fitz*. "How are you making out?" he asked.

"We are holding our own," replied Captain McSorley.

These were the last words heard from anyone aboard the *Edmund Fitzgerald*. A few minutes later something happened that no one who was on the *Anderson* bridge that day will ever forget. The *Fitzgerald*'s ghostly radar image faded from the *Anderson* screen just as it had done so many times throughout the afternoon. But this time it did not return. Seconds passed, then minutes, and still there was no sign of the *Fitzgerald*. Incredibly, a modern ship, as long as a sixty-story building is tall, had vanished in the blink of an eye.

How did it happen? We may never know. No survivors were ever found, and a concerted search by air and water turned up only a few scattered bits of debris: a wooden stool, a propane bottle, a shattered lifeboat, and little else. Many months would pass before the wreck itself was located. According to a Coast Guard survey of the site completed in the spring of 1976, the *Fitzgerald*'s hull lay in two pieces among mounds of rusting taconite some five hundred feet below the surface of Lake Superior. Some are of the opinion that the *Fitzgerald* was broken in half by a pair of huge waves that struck it simultaneously in the bow and the stern. Others think the ship took on too much water through her damaged deck hatches, slid down the side of a wave, and plunged to the bottom where she was broken apart by the impact. Still others believe the big freighter came too close to a shoal, struck bottom, and then slowly filled with water through a crack in her hull.

In 1980 a number of divers from Jacques Cousteau's famous research ship *Calypso* braved the lake's deep, blood-freezing waters to visit the *Fitzgerald* in her grave. Since then at least two robot submarines have taken photographs of the wreck. But none of these expeditions has shed much light on the cause of the disaster. To this day the *Fitzgerald* continues to guard her secrets jealously. All we know for certain is that the *Big Fitz* was sunk by one of Lake Superior's furious late autumn storms—what Gordon Lightfoot's ballad describes as "the Witch of November."

A Bell from the Big Fitz

Partly because of the Lightfoot ballad, the disaster that claimed the *Edmund Fitzgerald* has become a legend in our own time. Much has been written on it, and the wreck is occasionally mentioned in television documentaries. However, the most appropriate and certainly most enjoyable place to learn about the sinking of *Fitz* is on the banks of the very lake that swallowed it.

The wreck of the *Fitzgerald* lies about seventeen miles to the northwest of the light station at Whitefish Point, home of the Great Lakes Shipwreck Museum. Centerpiece of the museum is a bronze ship's bell engraved with the name EDMUND FITZGERALD. The bell is a fairly recent acquisition. It was recovered from the wreck during a 1995 diving expedition assisted by the National Geographic Society and the Canadian Navy.

"Family members who lost loved ones aboard the *Edmund Fitzgerald* asked us if we wouldn't return to the wreck and bring up an object that would really represent what the *Fitzgerald* was about," says Tom Farnquist, the director of the museum. "That was the bell."

Bell from the *Edmund Fitzgerald*

Tom Farnquist

Slightly distorted by a thin layer of mist and fog, this photograph shows **Whitefish Light Station,** on Lake Superior. The cast-iron tower was designed and built during the early days of the Civil War.

Each of the nearly ninety thousand visitors who pass through the museum every summer spends at least a few moments gazing at the bell brought up from the lightless, ice-cold waters hundreds of feet down in the lake. But there is plenty more to see here. Filled with glowing lighthouse lenses, diving equipment, and artifacts from dozens of wrecks, the museum is a delight for anyone interested in the rich history and lore of the lakes.

"We established this museum to share the excitement and adventure of diving to shipwrecks," says Farnquist. "And also to remember the sailors who were lost."

It is estimated that more than six thousand sships and other large vessels have been claimed by the Great Lakes. The number of lives lost in these wrecks is less certain, but surely it runs to many thousands. No doubt these losses would have been much larger if not for the lakes' extensive system of navigational lights.

The oldest light station on Lake Superior is the one right here at Whitefish Point. Established in 1848, it marks a strategic northeastward extension of Michigan's Upper Peninsula with protected waters lying to the south and east. Any ship hit by a storm in the eastern reaches of Superior will likely make a run for the relative calm of Whitefish Bay. Usually, they can follow the powerful Whitefish Point beacon to safety.

Ironically, on the night the *Fitzgerald* was lost, the Whitefish Point Light was not shining. The storm had knocked down electric lines and darkened the entire peninsula, including the Whitefish Point Station. Most believe this played no role in the *Fitzgerald* tragedy since the big ship never got close enough for its captain to see the beacon even if it had been in operation. Still it is a remarkable coincidence that the light was out of service on that particular evening. Otherwise, it has been extraordinarily reliable, and in a century and a half it has seldom been dark, even for as long a single night. Lake sailors have always been able to count on it just as they do today.

Originally, the beacon shone from atop a stone lighthouse of traditional design, but in 1861 President Abraham Lincoln ordered construction of the present eighty-foot-tall iron tower. It has an unexpectedly modern look.

Whitefish Point Light

"The tower surprises a lot of people," says Farnquist, who is often asked about the twentieth-century appearance of this Civil War–era lighthouse. "They take a look and they see this fairly well-engineered metal structure that went together something like an erector set."

The tower's central column is supported by four heavily braced legs. This open design, sometimes called a steel skeleton, allows storm winds to pass harmlessly through the structure rather than press against it. As a result, the Whitefish Point Lighthouse has survived even the most destructive gales.

The storms that lash the lakes combine with shallow water and shoals to make the stretch of Michigan shoreline to the west of Whitefish Point especially dangerous for ships. Of the approximately 550 large vessels sunk by Lake Superior, perhaps a third have met with disaster on or near the approximately one hundred miles of shore between Whitefish Point and Marquette.

"That's why it's called the Shipwreck Coast," says Farnquist.

About halfway along this deadly coast, at Grand Marais in Pictured Rocks National Lakeshore, the National Park Service maintains a small maritime museum. Like the museum at Whitefish Point, it focuses on shipwrecks. Here visitors will find displays and artifacts from many Great Lakes wrecks, including that of the *Fitzgerald*. Even the museum's rest rooms are historic. The *Fitzgerald*'s last messages were picked up by a radioman in a communications room once housed in this building. The room has now been subdivided into men's and women's toilets and signs inform visitors, "You are now seated in almost the same spot where the last message from the *Fitzgerald* was received."

Pharos of the Midwest

aving lives has always been the most important function of lighthouses, but they were also built to attract commerce. In the past a port city with a lighthouse had a distinct advantage over cities with poorly marked harbors. Trading ships were naturally drawn to ports that were easily found and safely approached.

"The great grandfather of all lighthouses was the Pharos, constructed by the Greeks about 285 B.C. at the port of Alexandria in Egypt," says historian Don Terrace, who lives at the Grosse Point Lighthouse in Evanston, Illinois. Terrace is the manager of the Grosse Point Historical Site.

Listed among the Seven Wonders of the World, the Pharos was said to stand more than four hundred feet tall. At night a bright fire was lit at the top of the great stone tower located on an island at the mouth of the Alexandria Harbor. This beacon attracted ships from all over the Mediterranean and helped make Alexandria the ancient world's most prosperous port. Greek and Roman freighters flocked to the city to load up on the grain grown in wondrous abundance in the rich soils of the Nile Delta. The giant lighthouse that guided them stood for more than a thousand years before being felled by an earthquake.

Like Alexandria, Chicago served as the gateway to a marvelously productive agricultural region. The city's first official lighthouse was built in 1831, but it proved far less durable than the Pharos. In what Terrace describes as a "tragedy with comic overtones," the wooden tower collapsed only hours after it was completed. The fallen tower was quickly rebuilt, however, since its

Don Terrace

Chicago Harbor Light

Grosse Point Light

light was desperately needed. Chicago was about to become one of the nation's most important ports. "Grain and food stuffs were going east out of Chicago, while the timber and supplies needed to build the West were flowing into Chicago," says Terrace.

Seen here through arching tree branches, the **Grosse Point Lighthouse** rises skyward over Evanston's Lake Michigan shoreline. This elegant tower dates to 1873.

For a time, during the late nineteenth century, Chicago's port vied with New York and San Francisco as the busiest in the country. Lines of freighters could be seen moving along the southwestern shores of Lake Michigan headed for the Windy City. Then, slowly but surely, most of the commercial maritime traffic shifted to other harbors to the north and south of Chicago. Today, the city's harbor is used primarily by pleasure boaters.

The lighthouse that guides vessels into the Chicago Harbor nowadays dates to 1893, the year of the renowned Columbian Exposition. On display at the fair was an especially fine third-order Fresnel lens, which had been intended for the Point Loma Lighthouse in southern California. At the end of the Exposition, federal lighthouse officials decided to leave the lens in Chicago as a public relations gesture. Its flashing red light can still be seen marking the end of a breakwater at the entrance to the harbor.

For many years the Chicago Harbor Light worked in tandem with a second beacon about a dozen miles to the north. Navigators of Chicago-bound ships looked first for the light shining from Grosse Point in Evanston and counted on it to lead them onward to the Chicago Harbor Light and the port.

"The Grosse Point Lighthouse was constructed to act as a guidepost for ships moving in and out of Chicago," says Terrace.

The graceful, 113-foot Grosse Point tower was completed in 1873. Like the Rock of Ages Lighthouse far to the north, it received an especially powerful second-order Fresnel lens. The station was also given a double-sized keeper's dwelling and several additional buildings to house the fog signal and other equipment. The Italianate residence was so spacious and comfortable and the amenities of upscale Evanston so inviting that keepers were anxious to be posted here by the Lighthouse Service.

"It was known as a very desirable, very plush station," says Terrace. "You had access to an affluent community and a good school system in Evanston, the home of Northwestern

University. It was nothing like being at the Rock of Ages Lighthouse or some station like that out in the middle of Lake Superior or Lake Michigan."

Terrace is well aware of the attractions of Grosse Point. For years now he has lived in the fine old keeper's quarters while serving as curator of the city-owned lighthouse museum. Having developed an interest in maritime anthropology while in graduate school, Terrace jumped at a chance to come to Grosse Point when a job opened up here in the mid-1980s. Since then he has developed what he describes as a "passion" for lighthouses and lighthouse preservation. "I feel strongly that, if historic lighthouses are to survive, they need to have a function," says Terrace. "The obvious function for most lighthouses would be as interpretive tools, as specialized maritime museums."

The effort to preserve the Grosse Point Lighthouse began shortly after it was decommissioned by the Lighthouse Service in 1934. The usefulness of the station and its light had declined along with the commercial lake traffic entering the Chicago Harbor. Fearing the station would be allowed to fall into ruin and become an eyesore, Evanston municipal officials asked the government to deed the property to the city. This was done the following year, and Evanston became one of the first cities in the country to own a lighthouse. Shortly after World War II, the beacon was re-lit as a private aid to navigation, and it has shone brightly ever since. The lighthouse survives today because it is viewed by the Evanston community as a cultural resource, an indispensable reminder of the past.

Lighthouse Park in the Apostles

In the far western reaches of Lake Superior, a cluster of twenty-two beautiful islands lie just off Wisconsin's Chequamegon Peninsula. Teeming with wildlife and steeped in history, these pristine fragments of an earlier, wilder America are recognized by naturalists and historians alike as a national treasure. Now managed and protected by the Park Service, the islands are an increasingly popular summer travel destination. And no wonder. In addition to their fine beaches, lush woodlands, and other natural attractions, they have something no other park can offer: half a dozen historic lighthouses all in excellent condition and most still in operation.

"People come here because there are campgrounds, fishing, and stuff," says Apostle Islands National Lakeshore historian Dave Snyder. "But there are also six great lighthouses out on the islands."

Arranged in a semicircle defining the dangerous outer edge of the Apostle

Michigan Island Light

Years ago, this modern plastic optic took the place of the original classical lens at **Outer Island** in the Apostles. Interestingly, this recently designed device employs old-fashioned Fresnel technology.

chain, the light stations are located on Raspberry Island, Sand Island, Outer Island, Devils Island, and Michigan Island, where there are two separate towers. Accessible by boat or ferry, they are all open to the public, and together they comprise what is in effect the nation's most extensive outdoor lighthouse museum.

"It's unusual to find so many lighthouses in such a concentrated area," says Synder. "We do a lot of research on them. We do the best we can to restore them, and to the public we say, 'Come on and have a look.'"

During warm weather months, the Park Service offers a variety of tours and interpretive services. Rangers and volunteer guides describe the architecture and history of towers, explain the technical aspects of using a lamp and lens to produce a lighthouse beacon, and even try to help visitors imagine what it was like to live and work in the Apostles as a lighthouse keeper.

Built over a period of about half a century, the various station buildings provide an interesting mix of architectural styles. "You've got a white stone tower on Michigan Island and a fancy brownstone one over on Sand Island," explains Snyder. "You've got the Queen Anne keeper's houses on Devil's Island that look like something you'd find in a midwestern streetcar suburb."

Visitors find the history of these lovely light stations as fascinating as it is diverse. Oldest of the Apostles lighthouses is the 1857 masonry tower and attached dwelling on Michigan Island. Oddly enough, the station was put here by mistake. It had been intended for nearby Long Island, but due perhaps to some miscommunication between government officials and the construction crew, it was built on Michigan Island instead. By the time inspectors discovered the error, the misplaced buildings were already standing on Michigan Island, and the Lighthouse Service decided to leave well enough alone.

Long Island eventually got its lighthouse also, a small wooden structure that served until 1895. Today, a tall metal light tower marks privately owned Long Island, which is the only part of the Apostles chain not managed by the Park Service. If Long Island were included within its boundaries, the Apostle Islands National Lakeshore could boast seven lighthouses rather than six.

Ironically, there are now two lighthouses on Michigan Island, which was never supposed to have one in the first place. The second, an eight-legged iron skeleton, was moved here from Maine's Schooner Ledge in 1930. Shipped halfway across the country in pieces, the 102-foot-tall

One of half a dozen historic lighthouses in the Apostle Islands off Wisconsin's Chequamegan Peninsula, the **Outer Island Light** station dates to 1874. The conical brick tower is 80 feet tall, but because of the elevation of the site, its beacon has a focal plane more than 130 feet above Lake Superior.

Although no longer an active aid to navigation, the **Raspberry Island Lighthouse** is a busy place during the summer, when a living-history program brings its past to life for tour groups.

cylinder and supporting steel framework was reassembled not far from the original station. The earlier lighthouse, by that time considered too old and too short to do its job efficiently, was then retired.

Also now in retirement is the red-roofed Raspberry Island Lighthouse. Built during the Civil War to guide vessels through the treacherous inner passage snaking between the islands, the wooden tower and dwelling remained in use for almost a hundred years. Then in 1957 the Coast Guard assigned the task of marking the channel to an automated pole-mounted light. Afterward, the station was closed, its lens removed, and its keepers sent elsewhere.

During the summer, volunteer Matt Welter entertains Raspberry Island visitors by dramatizing the history of the station. As part of a living-history interpretive program, Welter assumes the character of an assistant keeper who served here during the 1930s. "Alrighty folks, welcome to Raspberry Island," he says as visitors step off the park ferry. "My name is Toots Winfield." Little is known about the real Toots (Herbert) Winfield, a single man with few family ties and a mysterious background. It is said he loved children, and obviously, so does Welter. Dressed in an old-fashioned Lighthouse Service uniform, Welter

Matt Welter

delights young people and adults with his antics. Running up imaginary steps to check on the lamps and shoveling imaginary coal to fuel fog-signal boilers, he comically demonstrates how hard keepers had to work.

Welter makes everyone laugh with his ducklike imitation of a Gabriel's horn, a handheld signaling device used before steam foghorns were installed here. "Do this with me," he says, blowing through his hands, and the children, at least, make an effort.

"A three-second blast once a minute for as long as the fog held. Do you think you could do that all night long?" The children don't think so. "And if the boat kept coming, you'd get out the megaphone and yell, 'Hey, you yahoo, you're gonna hit my island!' "

Welter has done similar interpretive programs at the Grand Canyon and on Isle Royale, about a hundred miles northeast of the Apostles. He is a strong believer in the living-history approach to exploring the past. "There are little things we do and say to get ideas planted in peoples' minds," he explains. "We try not to give out just facts, because facts don't really say much. I can tell you that the lighthouse is forty feet high, or that the lighthouse is high enough that, if you fell off, you might break an arm or a leg. Which are you going to remember?"

Superior's Biggest Rock

Lighthouses are also an important attraction of Lake Superior's wild and remote Isle Royale National Park. The park embraces and protects one of the world's largest freshwater islands, a rugged blade of basaltic rock more than forty miles long. There are four lighthouses here, if one counts the Rock of Ages station several miles offshore. As is done in the Apostles, the National Park Service uses these structures as interpretive tools to help visitors explore the history of the island and the lake.

Summer visitors reach Isle Royale by way of ferries departing from Copper Harbor or Houghton on the Michigan Keweenah Peninsula. A one-way crossing on the lake's often choppy waters may take several hours. Passengers are nearly always happy to feel solid ground under their feet when they arrive at Rock Harbor on the island.

To the west of the landing is the 1855 Rock Harbor Lighthouse, a masonry tower with a small attached dwelling. Although its lantern has been dark for more than a century, the park service has put the old building to good use as a maritime museum.

"It's a great use for a structure like that," says ranger Elizabeth Valencia, the park's cultural historian. "It's an ideal place for a maritime history exhibit. When you look out, you

see the channel and you know why that lighthouse was put there."

The walls are covered with maps, charts, and historic photographs. Exhibits give visitors a look into the often stormy past of the lake and the island, once a copper-mining center. Open logbooks allow a glimpse into the lives of keepers who lived here with their families long ago. An entry in one of the logs reads: "May 19, 1886. The weather is very cold. We can hardly drink the water, it is so cold." Another reads: "We leave this afternoon half froze—10th November, 1886."

Rock Harbor Light

Increasingly, visitors are showing an interest in the park's other lighthouses as well, even though they are far more difficult to reach. One is on Managerie Island well out from Rock Harbor and near the entrance to Siskit Bay. Another is on Passage Island several miles to the east. The Rock of Ages Station is, of course, all but inaccessible.

"I think lighthouses have special meanings in different ways for lots of people," says Valencia. "Some people are very interested in the lighthouse building itself, the way it was built, where it was built, what shape it's in, the design, the light, the strength of the light, the size of the lens. They want to visit many different lighthouses and count the steps as they go to the top. Other people are more interested in the life of the light keeper. How did people live in those remote places? Where did they get their food? What did they do for fun? How were their lives different from the way we live now?"

Isle Royale makes a special effort to provide information on the keepers and not just the buildings where they lived and worked. "I think it's important to preserve not only the structure, but also the stories and feelings," says Valencia. "It's a way of life that's past now. If we don't preserve the lighthouses and if we don't get what information we can from the light keepers who are still alive, we'll lose it. That will be a missing part of our history."

Elizabeth Valencia

Now a National Park Service museum, the **Rock Harbor Lighthouse** once guided ore freighters to copper-rich Isle Royale in the northwestern reaches of Lake Superior. Keepers and their families lived here most of the year but went ashore during the winter when ice closed the lake to navigation.

Memories in Stone

For Anna Bowen Hoge the past is still very much alive at the Passage Island Lighthouse. Her father, Vernon Bowen, served as first assistant keeper here from 1930 to 1943, and this is where she spent her childhood. Now, after more than half a century, she has returned in search of an earlier time and an earlier self.

A pause at an upstairs window brings back a flood of memories. "This was my special place in the house," she recalls, gazing out at an expansive view of the island and the lake. "If I did something wrong and got sent to my room, that was great. I could sit in this window and watch."

Hoge had special places all over the island. In the rocks below the lighthouse, she cooked in an imaginary kitchen. Even now she has no trouble finding it and still remembers the layout. "See the stove," she says, pointing to a waist-high table of rock. "Just the right height. Notice it's got burners that are hot. It's got little shelves and make-believe salt and peppers. Right over here was water, and that was our sink."

Because she lived on this faraway island, Hoge did not see the inside of a school until she was ten years old. Nonetheless, she feels she missed little in the way of an education. "What they taught me here was very important," she says. "Education was part of what I called home. Learning to walk was learning to swim, learning safety, learning to respect Lake Superior."

Passage Island Light

Anna Hoge

Keeper Bowen and his family had no choice but to respect the lake. It influenced nearly every aspect of their daily lives. All supplies and mail came by way of the lake, and of course, the only way to reach the mainland was by boat. When cold winds or storms blew in off the lake, there was nothing to do but shutter the windows and wait for a break in the weather.

"Lake Superior is a lady," says Hoge. "When she's calm, she's beautiful, and you can enjoy her. But when she's mad and kicks up her heels, then you get into a safe port. You stay away from her."

Hoge regards her life here—the storms and the isolation as well as her special places and make-believe kitchen—as a gift. "You see, being here wasn't a duty," she says. "It was a way of life. It was something we were all proud of because of my father."

She has fond memories of her father climbing a ladder every morning to put up the station flag. Her eyes grow moist now at the sight of the Stars and Stripes flying over the stone walls of the Passage Island Lighthouse.

"It doesn't take much to carry you back," she says. "Or to bring you forward."

Sand Castle

Bill Frabotta

Sand Hills Light

The automated lights now in use along all of America's coasts do not require the constant attention of men such as Vernon Bowen. Family light stations, including the one Ann Hoge grew up in at Passage Island, no longer exist. However, it is possible to get a taste of the lighthouse experience, if only for a weekend, at an inn such as the one at Sand Hills on Lake Superior's Keweenah Peninsula.

Sand Hills is the largest lighthouse ever built on the Great Lakes. "Three lighthouse keepers and their families lived here," says Bill Frabotta, owner and keeper of the Sand Hills Inn, a bed-and-breakfast. "Each of the wings contains a kitchen, living room, dining room, three bedrooms, and a bathroom. The tower is seven levels to the top—101 feet above the water."

The massive, reinforced concrete tower and dwellings were built near the end of World War I to mark Sawtooth Reef lying just offshore. In 1910 the freighter *Moreland* struck the reef and sank, and this disaster led to construction of the lighthouse. Retired by the Coast Guard in 1954, Sand Hills no longer serves as an active navigational station. The lantern atop its squared-off tower is empty, but not so the old keepers quarters. Frabotta keeps them filled them with guests.

Frabotta bought the abandoned station in the 1980s and decided to restore it for use as an inn. But the project turned out to be much more of a challenge than he had expected. "This place was in shambles," he says. "It was a mess."

After it was abandoned by the Coast Guard in 1947, the **Round Island Lighthouse** in the Straits of Mackinac fell into disrepair. It is now being restored, partly with the help of energetic Boy Scouts.

Years of work and thousands of dollars went into shoring up walls and refurbishing rooms. Frabotta's friends made bets on whether the restoration would ever be completed, and by 1993 it had begun to look as if it might not. But that year the would-be innkeeper decided to make one last, all-out effort. "I had to sell my home, my studio, my commercial building—even my Harley," he says. "I said, 'I'm gonna do it.' And I did it."

Now a carved blue and purple sign hangs outside the front entrance. It says SAND HILLS LIGHTHOUSE INN, FIVE MILE POINT, KEEPER WILLIAM H. FRABOTTA.

The inn's spacious rooms are popular with summer travelers seeking a view of the lake, some peace and quiet, and a unique experience. "People are thrilled to stay in a lighthouse," says Frabotta. "To hear the seagulls or the water and enjoy the majesty of Lake Superior. And sooner or later, of course, they head for the tower."

There is no lamp in the Sand Hills tower nowadays, but that doesn't seem to bother Frabotta's guests. The view from the top is as awe inspiring as the old building itself is endlessly engaging.

"Lighthouses are the castles of America," says one Sand Hills guest. "They sit out on these strange peninsulas, and people get curious about them and want to experience them for themselves."

Lighthouse Friends

Guests at the Grand Hotel on Mackinac Island in the straits of Mackinac have been known to compare the place to a European castle. The horse-and-buggy charm of this century-old resort is distinctly old world and has helped make it a magnet for tourists since not long after the Civil War. The island bans automobiles, so visitors must get around on foot or in carriages, but few complain about the relaxed pace. Most are content to take a few turns on one of the lush bowling greens or just relax in a comfortable chair.

The rockers on what must be nearly an acre of front porch allow guests to gaze out across the straits. To the south is the lower Michigan Peninsula, to the north, the Upper Peninsula, and due west, the Mackinac Bridge, providing the only highway connection between the two. The straits themselves are a heavily trafficked liquid highway linking Lake Michigan with Lake Huron and the other lakes. So there is plenty to watch—pleasure boats coming and going from Mackinac Island or tankers and container ships rolling through on their way to Green Bay or Chicago.

One thing sure to catch a visitor's eye is the red-and-white Round Island Lighthouse, which guards an S-shaped spit of sand and gravel near the Mackinac Island Harbor entrance.

191

A two-and-one-half-story brick residence with a square tower rising just above the roof line, it was built in 1895 to guide vessels through the straits. Staffed by three, full-time keepers, who worked in shifts around the clock, the station served for more than half a century.

Then, in 1947, the Coast Guard established an automated light farther out in the straits and abandoned the lighthouse. Years of neglect left it a ruin, and in 1972 storm-driven waves broke through the lower walls, stopping just short of washing the old light station away. With the foundation crumbling, it seemed certain the building would soon collapse into the lake. The U.S. Forest Service, which had owned the lighthouse since the 1950s, decided to tear it down.

At this point a group of five local residents banded together to save the historic struc-

Dick Moehl

ture. Calling themselves the Friends of the Round Island Lighthouse, they managed to get the building listed on the National Register of Historic Places and then pressured the Forest Service until the agency agreed to leave it standing. The lake itself, however, could not be turned aside so easily. Unless something was done, and done quickly, high winter waters were sure to demolish the lighthouse.

"We didn't have a penny," says Gary Myron, a charter Friends member. But somehow the little organization managed to convince a contractor, working on long-term credit, to dump tons of heavy stone riprap around the building.

Round Island Light

"That's really what kept it standing through that first winter," says Myron. "That's what saved it. But it took us a good long time to finish paying for all that riprap."

In fact, it took the Friends nearly twenty years to pay off the debt. To raise money, they sold buttons and T-shirts that said I'M A ROUND ISLAND LIGHTHOUSE KEEPER. Any money that could be spared went into restoration of the sadly deteriorated dwelling and tower.

Over the years, other groups have gotten involved in the project. One of these is the Great Lakes Lighthouse Keepers Association, an organization committed to salvaging lighthouses and other decaying reminders of the region's maritime heritage. Formed in 1983, the association consists of educators, preservationists, and old-time keepers who actually served at the lights.

Every summer, Association president Dick Moehl brings boatloads of Boy Scouts to Round Island to help restore the old building. Scouts from Freeland, Michigan, Troop 323 earn merit badges for working here. "Sort of a Huck Finn experience," Moehl says of the Boy Scout outings. "We have fun." Moehl feels that involving young people is a vital part of the restoration process. "That way we're developing a new generation of preservationists," he says.

Despite the enthusiasm and boundless energies of the young scouts, however, the work at Round Island is moving ahead very slowly. The job is too big for one or even several seasons. Moehl believes a complete restoration may take ten more years. "You look at the whole thing and you say it can't be done," he says. "But as soon as you say let's do it one room at a time or one inch at a time, then all of a sudden it becomes manageable."

Dale Gensman is another one who takes a step-by-step approach to preservation. A carpenter who restores woodwork in historic buildings, Gensman is now doing the same for the Round Island Lighthouse. All the wooden supports and surfaces inside the station are being repaired and refitted with meticulous attention to detail. Even the sunbursts, carved into the wood as a sort of signature by the original carpenters, are being reworked.

"If people are going to come over here and visit, they're entitled to see how it originally looked," says Gensman. "It's going to look like the day it was put here. It's all oak and should finish up very nicely." Gensman sees the work as a memorial for his father, who did some of the carpentry here when the station was built in 1895. "I wanted to give something back to him. I thought this was the way to do it."

Lamp in a Window

On the northeastern shore of Lake Michigan, the long dormant Grand Traverse Lighthouse is enjoying a new life under the care of a special keeper. Boarded up after the station was shut down by the Coast Guard in the 1970s, the lighthouse has now been handsomely restored and opened to the public. Visitors are shown through the 140-year-old building by Doug McCormick, a retired coastguardsman and ferry

Doug McCormick

pilot. McCormick's claim on this job is a strong one. He grew up here.

"I came here when I was nine years old," says McCormick, whose father became keeper of the Grand Traverse Light in 1922. McCormick was born at the lighthouse on Poverty Island in Wisconsin and spent part of his childhood at the Fox Island Station about seventeen miles from Grand Traverse. His grandfather had been a keeper, and his father devoted more than thirty years to the Lighthouse Service. The McCormicks were a lighthouse family.

Established in 1853, the **Grand Traverse Light Station** was shut down during the 1970s. Carefully restored, it is now part of a Michigan state park. Visitors are shown through the building by a retired coastguardsman who lived here during the 1920s when his father served as keeper.

Walking through the station with visitors, McCormick brings it to life for them. "There was no electricity—it was all kerosene back then, " he says. "We had two pair of long johns. One was in the wash, and you wore the other until you changed on Saturday."

"Whether you needed to or not," pipes in a helpful tourist.

"That's right," McCormick agrees.

For McCormick, leading a tour of this lighthouse means taking a stroll through his past. The place is furnished with his own family heirlooms. He is especially proud of the organ in the parlor. "This organ has quite a history," McCormick says. "My mother got it in 1899 when my father gave it to her as a wedding present."

The **St. Helena Lighthouse** in Lake Michigan is now in the care of the Great Lakes Lighthouse Keepers Association. During the summer, Boy Scouts earn credit toward merit badges by helping with restoration work. The 71-foot brick tower was built in 1871.

The old lighthouse itself has quite a history. While under construction during the early 1850s, it became the target of a bizarre raid by followers of a Mormon zealot who had proclaimed himself king of a nearby island. Undeterred by the Old Testament Commandment "Thou shalt not steal," the raiders grabbed everything that could be moved, including parts for the station's vital lighting apparatus. However, before they could make off with their booty, they ran head-on into a frontier lawman. The station's keeper, Philo Beers, was also a U.S. deputy marshal, and he drove them off in a blaze of gunfire.

Completed in 1853, the station stood on Cat Head Point from which it guided ships into strategic Grand Traverse Bay. Its fourth-order Fresnel lens beamed out over Lake Michigan from atop a square tower and lantern room rising through the pitched roof of the two-story dwelling. The station operated continuously until 1972, when the job of lighting the entrance to the bay was given to a small skeleton tower, which proved much easier and less expensive to maintain.

During its nearly 120 years of service, several generations of lighthouse keepers and their families made a home of the lighthouse. The McCormicks found their life here congenial if not always comfortable.

"We had a sing-along a couple of times a week," recalls McCormick. "My mother would play the organ and my father played a zither. I played a harmonica and my brother played a guitar. And I had three sisters who were really good singers. It was a happy time. A family time."

Now the lighthouse is once again McCormick's home. He keeps the rooms neat, the flower boxes outside carefully weeded, and everything shipshape just as his father and mother did so long ago. And for those who may be lost in the dark, he keeps a light burning, if only an ordinary lamp in an upstairs window.

McCormick knows that lighthouses are no longer essential for navigation. They are, in fact, all too dispensable. But he also understands that, even if for different reasons, we need these venerable structures as much as we ever did. And unless we care for them, they will be gone. We are the keepers now, and only time will tell how well we do our jobs.

Index

Numerals in italic indicate photograph only.

About the Authors

John Grant is president and executive producer of Driftwood Productions, Inc. He created and executive produced the *Legendary Lighthouses* television series for PBS. Driftwood Productions has also produced the six-part *America's Scenic Rail Journeys* and *The Rockies by Rail* for public television. Prior to Driftwood Productions, Grant was senior vice president of national programming at the Public Broadcasting Service (PBS) in Alexandria, Virginia. He also spent sixteen years at WPSX-TV, the public television station at Penn State University. Grant lives with his wife, Joan, and son, Andy, in Burke, Virginia.

Ray Jones is a freelance writer and publishing consultant living in Surry, a small town on the coast of Maine. He is the text author of all eight books in Globe Pequot's popular Lighthouses series. Jones began his writing career working as a reporter for weekly newspapers in Texas. Since then he has served as an editor for Time-Life Books, as founding editor of *Albuquerque Living* magazine, as a senior editor and writing coach at *Southern Living* magazine, and as founder and publisher of Country Roads Press.

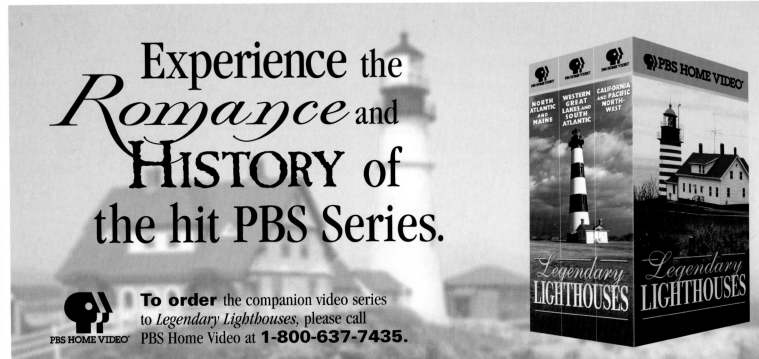